MznLnx

Missing Links Exam Preps

Exam Prep for

Principles of Microeconomics

Case & Fair, 7th Edition

The MznLnx Exam Prep is your link from the texbook and lecture to your exams.
The MznLnx Exam Preps are unauthorized and comprehensive reviews of your textbooks.

All material provided by MznLnx and Rico Publications (c) 2010
Textbook publishers and textbook authors do not particpate in or contribute to these reviews.

MznLnx

Rico
Publications

Exam Prep for Principles of Microeconomics
7th Edition
Case & Fair

Publisher: Raymond Houge
Assistant Editor: Michael Rouger
Text and Cover Designer: Lisa Buckner
Marketing Manager: Sara Swagger
Project Manager, Editorial Production: Jerry Emerson
Art Director: Vernon Lowerui

Product Manager: Dave Mason
Editorial Assitant: Rachel Guzmanji
Pedagogy: Debra Long
Cover Image: Jim Reed/Getty Images
Text and Cover Printer: City Printing, Inc.
Compositor: Media Mix, Inc.

(c) 2010 Rico Publications
ALL RIGHTS RESERVED. No part of this work covered by the copyright may be reproduced or used in any form or by an means--graphic, electronic, or mechanical, including photocopying, recording, taping, Web distribution, information storage, and retrieval systems, or in any other manner--without the written permission of the publisher.

Printed in the United States
ISBN:

For more information about our products, contact us at:
Dave.Mason@RicoPublications.com

For permission to use material from this text or product, submit a request online to:
Dave.Mason@RicoPublications.com

Contents

CHAPTER 1
The Scope and Method of Economics — 1

CHAPTER 2
The Economic Problem: Scarcity and Choice — 12

CHAPTER 3
Demand, Supply, and Market Equilibrium — 20

CHAPTER 4
Demand and Supply Applications and Elasticity — 27

CHAPTER 5
Household Behavior and Consumer Choice — 34

CHAPTER 6
The Production Process: The Behavior of Profit-Maximizing Firms — 43

CHAPTER 7
Short-Run Costs and Output Decisions — 48

CHAPTER 8
Long-Run Costs and Output Decisions — 53

CHAPTER 9
Input Demand: The Labor and Land Markets — 58

CHAPTER 10
Input Demand: The Capital Market and the Investment Decision — 64

CHAPTER 11
General Equilibrium and the Efficiency of Perfect Competition — 71

CHAPTER 12
Monopoly and Antitrust Policy — 77

CHAPTER 13
Monopolistic Competition and Oligopoly — 87

CHAPTER 14
Externalities, Public Goods, Imperfect Information, and Social Choice — 96

CHAPTER 15
Income Distribution and Poverty — 106

CHAPTER 16
Public Finance: The Economics of Taxation — 116

CHAPTER 17
International Trade, Comparative Advantage, and Protectionism — 123

CHAPTER 18
Globalization — 130

CHAPTER 19
Economic Growth in Developing and Transitional Economies — 137

ANSWER KEY — 149

TO THE STUDENT

COMPREHENSIVE

The *MznLnx* Exam Prep series is designed to help you pass your exams. Editors at MznLnx review your textbooks and then prepare these practice exams to help you master the textbook material. Unlike study guides, workbooks, and practice tests provided by the texbook publisher and textbook authors, *MznLnx* gives you **all** of the material in each chapter in exam form, not just samples, so you can be sure to nail your exam.

MECHANICAL

The MznLnx Exam Prep series creates exams that will help you learn the subject matter as well as test you on your understanding. Each question is designed to help you master the concept. Just working through the exams, you gain an understanding of the subject--its a simple mechanical process that produces success.

INTEGRATED STUDY GUIDE AND REVIEW

MznLnx is not just a set of exams designed to test you, its also a comprehensive review of the subject content. Each exam question is also a review of the concept, making sure that you will get the answer correct without having to go to other sources of material. You learn as you go! Its the easiest way to pass an exam.

HUMOR

Studying can be tedious and dry. MznLnx's instructional design includes moderate humor within the exam questions on occassion, to break the tedium and revitalize the brain

Chapter 1. The Scope and Method of Economics

1. _____s is the social science that studies the production, distribution, and consumption of goods and services. The term _____s comes from the Ancient Greek oá¼°κονομῖα from oá¼¶κος (oikos, 'house') + vΐŒμος (nomos, 'custom' or 'law'), hence 'rules of the house(hold)'. Current _____ models developed out of the broader field of political economy in the late 19th century, owing to a desire to use an empirical approach more akin to the physical sciences.
    a. Opportunity cost
    b. Inflation
    c. Energy economics
    d. Economic

2. _____ is a branch of economics that deals with the performance, structure, and behavior of a national or regional economy as a whole. Along with microeconomics, _____ is one of the two most general fields in economics. It is the study of the behavior and decision-making of entire economies.
    a. Tobit model
    b. Nominal value
    c. New Trade Theory
    d. Macroeconomics

3. _____ is a branch of economics that studies how individuals, households and firms and some states make decisions to allocate limited resources, typically in markets where goods or services are being bought and sold. _____ examines how these decisions and behaviours affect the supply and demand for goods and services, which determines prices; and how prices, in turn, determine the supply and demand of goods and services.

Whereas macroeconomics involves the 'sum total of economic activity, dealing with the issues of growth, inflation and unemployment, and with national economic policies relating to these issues' and the effects of government actions on them.

    a. Microeconomics
    b. Countercyclical
    c. Recession
    d. New Keynesian economics

4. _____ or economic opportunity loss is the value of the next best alternative foregone as the result of making a decision. _____ analysis is an important part of a company's decision-making processes but is not treated as an actual cost in any financial statement. The next best thing that a person can engage in is referred to as the _____ of doing the best thing and ignoring the next best thing to be done.
    a. Industrial organization
    b. Economic ideology
    c. Economic
    d. Opportunity cost

5. _____ is the use of marginal concepts within economics. (Marginal concepts are associated with a specific change in the quantity used of a good or of a service, as opposed to some notion of the over-all significance of that class of good or service, or of some total quantity thereof.) The central concept of _____ proper is that of marginal utility, but marginalists following the lead of Alfred Marshall were further heavily dependent upon the concept of marginal physical productivity in their explanation of cost; and the neoclassical tradition that emerged from British _____ generally abandoned the concept of utility and gave marginal rates of substitution a more fundamental rôle in analysis.
    a. Just price
    b. Marginalism
    c. Tendency of the rate of profit to fall
    d. Classical economics

6. In economics and business decision-making, _____ are costs that cannot be recovered once they have been incurred. _____ are sometimes contrasted with variable costs, which are the costs that will change due to the proposed course of action, and prospective costs which are costs that will be incurred if an action is taken.

In traditional microeconomic theory, only variable costs are relevant to a decision.

Chapter 1. The Scope and Method of Economics

a. Sunk costs
b. Hyperbolic discounting
c. Halo effect
d. Post-purchase rationalization

7. In management accounting, _____ establishes budget and actual cost of operations, processes, departments or product and the analysis of variances, profitability or social use of funds. Managers use _____ to support decision-making to cut a company's costs and improve profitability. As a form of management accounting, _____ need not follow standards such as GAAP, because its primary use is for internal managers, rather than outside users, and what to compute is instead decided pragmatically.

a. Total absorption costing
b. Quality costs
c. Khozraschyot
d. Cost accounting

8. _____ was a survey conducted by the U.S. Department of Justice to gauge the prevalence of alcohol and illegal drug use among prior arrestees. It was a reformulation of the prior Drug Use Forecasting (DUF) program, focused on five drugs in particular: cocaine, marijuana, methamphetamine, opiates, and PCP.

Participants were randomly selected from arrest records in major metropolitan areas; because no personally identifying information is taken from each record chosen, the resulting data can be correlated to arrest rates, but not to the total population of persons charged.

a. ACEA agreement
b. Arrestee Drug Abuse Monitoring
c. ACCRA Cost of Living Index
d. AD-IA Model

9. The _____ was a period in the late 18th and early 19th centuries when major changes in agriculture, manufacturing, mining, and transportation had a profound effect on the socioeconomic and cultural conditions in Britain. The changes subsequently spread throughout Europe, North America, and eventually the world. The onset of the _____ marked a major turning point in human society; almost every aspect of daily life was eventually influenced in some way.

a. Adolph Fischer
b. Adolf Hitler
c. Adam Smith
d. Industrial Revolution

10.

_____ was a German philosopher, political economist, historian, political theorist, sociologist, communist and revolutionary credited as the founder of communism.

Marx summarized his approach to history and politics in the opening line of the first chapter of The Communist Manifesto : e;The history of all hitherto existing society is the history of class struggles.e; Marx argued that capitalism, like previous socioeconomic systems, will produce internal tensions which will lead to its destruction. Just as capitalism replaced feudalism, socialism will in its turn replace capitalism and lead to a stateless, classless society which will emerge after a transitional period, the 'dictatorship of the proletariat'.

a. Adam Smith
b. Marxism
c. Karl Heinrich Marx
d. Neo-Gramscianism

11. _____ was a Scottish moral philosopher and a pioneer of political economy. One of the key figures of the Scottish Enlightenment, Smith is the author of The Theory of Moral Sentiments and An Inquiry into the Nature and Causes of the Wealth of Nations. The latter, usually abbreviated as The Wealth of Nations, is considered his magnum opus and the first modern work of economics.

   a. Alan Greenspan   b. Adolph Fischer
   c. Adolf Hitler   d. Adam Smith

12. An Inquiry into the Nature and Causes of the _____ is the magnum opus of the Scottish economist Adam Smith. It is a clearly written account of economics at the dawn of the Industrial Revolution, as well as a rhetorical piece written for the generally educated individual of the 18th century - advocating a free market economy as more productive and more beneficial to society.

The work is credited as a watershed in history and economics due to its comprehensive, largely accurate characterization of economic mechanisms that survive in modern economics; and also for its effective use of rhetorical technique, including structuring the work to contrast real world examples of free and fettered markets.

   a. The Rise and Fall of the Great Powers   b. The Bell Curve
   c. Black Book of Communism   d. Wealth of Nations

13. The _____ is the official currency of 16 of the 27 member states of the European Union (EU.) The states, known collectively as the Eurozone, are Austria, Belgium, Cyprus, Finland, France, Germany, Greece, Ireland, Italy, Luxembourg, Malta, the Netherlands, Portugal, Slovakia, Slovenia, and Spain. The currency is also used in a further five European countries, with and without formal agreements and is consequently used daily by some 327 million Europeans.

   a. Import and Export Price Indices   b. Equity capital market
   c. IRS Code 3401   d. Euro

14. The _____ is an economic and political union of 27 member states, located primarily in Europe. It was established by the Treaty of Maastricht on 1 November 1993, upon the foundations of the pre-existing European Economic Community. With a population of almost 500 million, the _____ generates an estimated 30% share (US$18.4 trillion in 2008) of the nominal gross world product.

   a. ACCRA Cost of Living Index   b. European Union
   c. ACEA agreement   d. European Court of Justice

15. The _____ or gross domestic income (GDI), a basic measure of an economy's economic performance, is the market value of all final goods and services produced within the borders of a nation in a year. _____ can be defined in three ways, all of which are conceptually identical. First, it is equal to the total expenditures for all final goods and services produced within the country in a stipulated period of time (usually a 365-day year.)

   a. Monopolistic competition   b. Countercyclical
   c. Market structure   d. Gross domestic product

16. In economics, _____ is a rise in the general level of prices of goods and services in an economy over a period of time. When the general price level rises, each unit of currency buys fewer goods and services; consequently, _____ is also a decline in the real value of money--a loss of purchasing power in the medium of exchange which is also the monetary unit of account in the economy. A chief measure of general price-level _____ is the general _____ rate, which is the percentage change in a general price index (normally the Consumer Price Index) over time.

a. Opportunity cost
b. Energy economics
c. Inflation
d. Economic

17. The Organization of the Petroleum Exporting Countries is a cartel of twelve countries made up of Algeria, Angola, Ecuador, Iran, Iraq, Kuwait, Libya, Nigeria, Qatar, Saudi Arabia, the United Arab Emirates, and Venezuela. The cartel has maintained its headquarters in Vienna since 1965, and hosts regular meetings among the oil ministers of its Member Countries. Indonesia withdrew its membership in _____ in 2008 after it became a net importer of oil, but stated it would likely return if it became a net exporter in the world.
a. ACCRA Cost of Living Index
b. ACEA agreement
c. OPEC
d. AD-IA Model

18. _____ is a misspelled phrase from Latin 'pro capite' phrase meaning per head with pro meaning 'per' or 'for each' and capite meaning 'head.' Both words together equate to the phrase 'for each head.'

It is usually used in the field of statistics to indicate the average per person for any given concern, such as income, crime rate, etc.

It is also used in wills to indicate that each of the named beneficiaries should receive, by devise or bequest, equal shares of the estate. This is in contrast to a per stirpes division, in which each branch of the inheriting family inherits an equal share of the estate.

a. Sargan test
b. Population statistics
c. False positive rate
d. Per capita

19. _____ means how much each individual receives, in monetary terms, of the yearly income generated in the country. This is what each citizen is to receive if the yearly national income is divided equally among everyone. _____ is usually reported in units of currency per year.
a. Family income
b. Real income
c. Lerman ratio
d. Per capita income

20. In economics, a _____ is a general slowdown in economic activity over a sustained period of time, or a business cycle contraction. During _____s, many macroeconomic indicators vary in a similar way. Production as measured by Gross Domestic Product (GDP), employment, investment spending, capacity utilization, household incomes and business profits all fall during _____s.
a. Leading indicators
b. Monetary economics
c. Treasury View
d. Recession

21. To _____ is to impose a financial charge or other levy upon a taxpayer by a state or the functional equivalent of a state.

_____es are also imposed by many subnational entities. _____es consist of direct _____ or indirect _____, and may be paid in money or as its labour equivalent (often but not always unpaid.)

a. 130-30 fund
b. 1921 recession
c. 100-year flood
d. Tax

22. _____ is the branch of economics that incorporates value judgments (that is, normative judgements) about what the economy ought to be like or what particular policy actions ought to be recommended to achieve a desirable goal. _____ looks at the desirability of certain aspects of the economy. It underlies expressions of support for particular economic policies.
   a. Normative economics
   b. Double bottom line
   c. Broad money
   d. Nanoeconomics

23. _____ is the branch of economics that concerns the description and explanation of economic phenomena (Wong, 1987, p. 920.) It focuses on facts and cause-and-effect relationships and includes the development and testing of economics theories.
   a. 100-year flood
   b. 130-30 fund
   c. Regulatory economics
   d. Positive economics

24. _____ is the subfield of economics dealing with the comparative study of different systems of economic organization, such as capitalism, socialism, feudalism and the mixed economy.

The comparative study of economic systems was of significant practical and political significance during the Cold War, when the relative merits of capitalist and communist systems of economic and political organization were a central topic of political concern. One of the most important early contributions was the calculation debate regarding the assertion of Ludwig von Mises that a system of central planning could never work because the information generated by a price system would never be available to planners.

   a. Market-based instruments
   b. Cost underestimation
   c. Comparative economic systems
   d. Black-Litterman model

25. _____s is concerned with the tasks of developing and applying quantitative or statistical methods to the study and elucidation of economic principles. _____s combines economic theory with statistics to analyze and test economic relationships. Theoretical _____s considers questions about the statistical properties of estimators and tests, while applied _____s is concerned with the application of _____ methods to assess economic theories.
   a. Economic
   b. Experimental economics
   c. Evolutionary economics
   d. Econometric

26. _____ is the development of economic wealth of countries or regions for the well-being of their inhabitants. It is the process by which a nation improves the economic, political, and social well being of its people. From a policy perspective, _____ can be defined as efforts that seek to improve the economic well-being and quality of life for a community by creating and/or retaining jobs and supporting or growing incomes and the tax base.
   a. Economic development
   b. Inflation
   c. Economic methodology
   d. Experimental economics

27. _____ is a field of economics that studies the strategic behavior of firms, the structure of markets and their interactions. The study of _____ adds to the perfectly competitive model real-world frictions such as limited information, transaction cost, cost of adjusting prices, government actions, and barriers to entry by new firms into a market. It then considers how firms are organized and how they compete.
   a. Economic ideology
   b. Industrial organization
   c. Inflation
   d. Economic

Chapter 1. The Scope and Method of Economics

28. _____ is a branch of economics with three main subdisciplines international trade, monetary economics and international finance.

- International trade studies goods-and-services flows across international boundaries from supply-and-demand factors, economic integration, and policy variables such as tariff rates and trade quotas.
- International finance studies the flow of capital across international financial markets, and the effects of these movements on exchange rates.
- International monetary economics and macroeconomics studies money and macro flows across countries.
- Stanley W. Black (2008.) 'international monetary institutions,' The New Palgrave Dictionary of Economics. 2nd Edition.

a. Economic depreciation
b. Index number
c. ACCRA Cost of Living Index
d. International economics

29. _____ is an approach to legal theory that applies methods of economics to law. It includes the use of economic concepts to explain the effects of laws, to assess which legal rules are economically efficient, and to predict which legal rules will be promulgated.

As used by lawyers and legal scholars, the phrase '_____' refers to the application of the methods of economics to legal problems.

a. Law and economics
b. Monopolistic competition
c. Public economics
d. Georgism

30. _____ is the study of economic issues concerning the public sector (including government) and its interface with the private sector (including households, businesses, and markets) in a mixed economy. While much of economics is based on how markets work, _____ considers the functioning of government and its role and scope in promoting economic well-being.

Broad methods and topics include:

- analysis and design of public policy
- public-finance theory and its application
- distributional effects of taxation and government expenditures
- analysis of market failure and government failure.

Emphasis is on analytical and scientific methods and normative-ethical analysis, as distinguished from ideology. Examples of topics covered are tax incidence, optimal taxation, the theory of public goods.

a. Nominal value
b. Public economics
c. Macroeconomics
d. Financial economics

31. _____ is broadly the economic study of urban areas. As such, it involves using the tools of economics to analyze urban issues such as crime, education, public transit, housing, and local government finance. More narrowly, it is a branch of microeconomics that studies urban spatial structure and the location of households and firms.

a. ACEA agreement
b. Urban economics
c. AD-IA Model
d. ACCRA Cost of Living Index

32. An _____ or Ã"conomic system is a system that involves the production, distribution and consumption of goods and services between the entities in a particular society. It is the method used by society to produce and distribute goods and services. The _____ is composed of people and institutions, including their relationships to productive resources, such as through the convention of property.
   a. Intention economy
   b. Information economy
   c. Indicative planning
   d. Economic system

33. The _____, a unit of the United States Department of Labor, is the principal fact-finding agency for the U.S. government in the broad field of labor economics and statistics. The BLS is an independent national statistical agency that collects, processes, analyzes, and disseminates essential statistical data to the American public, the U.S. Congress, other Federal agencies, State and local governments, business, and labor representatives. The BLS also serves as a statistical resource to the Department of Labor.
   a. Bureau of Labor Statistics
   b. Gross Regional Product
   c. Gross world product
   d. Gross national product

34. A _____ is the procedure of systematically acquiring and recording information about the members of a given population. It is a regularly occurring and official count of a particular population. The term is used mostly in connection with national 'population and door to door _____es' (to be taken every 10 years according to United Nations recommendations), agriculture, and business _____es.
   a. 1921 recession
   b. 100-year flood
   c. 130-30 fund
   d. Census

35. _____ is a broad label that refers to any individuals or households that use goods and services generated within the economy. The concept of a _____ is used in different contexts, so that the usage and significance of the term may vary.

Typically when business people and economists talk of _____s they are talking about person as _____, an aggregated commodity item with little individuality other than that expressed in the buy/not-buy decision.

   a. 100-year flood
   b. 1921 recession
   c. 130-30 fund
   d. Consumer

36. In economics, a model is a theoretical construct that represents economic processes by a set of variables and a set of logical and/or quantitative relationships between them. The _____ is a simplified framework designed to illustrate complex processes, often but not always using mathematical techniques. Frequently, _____s use structural parameters.
   a. ACCRA Cost of Living Index
   b. AD-IA Model
   c. Economic model
   d. ACEA agreement

37. In economics, the people in the _____ are the suppliers of labor. The _____ is all the nonmilitary people who are employed or unemployed. In 2005, the worldwide _____ was over 3 billion people.

a. Grenelle agreements
b. Distributed workforce
c. Departmentalization
d. Labor Force

38. In economics, the _____ is an economic law that states that consumers buy more of a good when its price decreases and less when its price increases.

There are certain goods which do not follow this law. These include Veblen and Giffen goods

a. Financial crisis
b. Law of demand
c. Market failure
d. Georgism

39. _____ was a predominant American integrated oil producing, transporting, refining, and marketing company. Established in 1870 as an Ohio Corporation, it was the largest oil refiner in the world and operated as a major company trust and was one of the world's first and largest multinational corporations until it was broken up by the United States Supreme Court in 1911. John D. Rockefeller was a founder, chairman and major shareholder, and the company made him a billionaire and eventually the richest man in history.

a. 100-year flood
b. 1921 recession
c. 130-30 fund
d. Standard Oil

40. Economics:

- _____, the desire to own something and the ability to pay for it
- _____ curve, a graphic representation of a _____ schedule
- _____ deposit, the money in checking accounts
- _____ pull theory, the theory that inflation occurs when _____ for goods and services exceeds existing supplies
- _____ schedule, a table that lists the quantity of a good a person will buy it each different price
- _____ side economics, the school of economics at believes government spending and tax cuts open economy by raising _____

a. Variability
b. McKesson ' Robbins scandal
c. Production
d. Demand

41. CÄ"terÄ«s paribus is a Latin phrase, literally translated as 'with other things the same.' It is commonly rendered in English as 'all other things being equal.' A prediction, or a statement about causal or logical connections between two states of affairs, is qualified by _____ in order to acknowledge, and to rule out, the possibility of other factors which could override the relationship between the antecedent and the consequent.

A _____ assumption is often fundamental to the predictive purpose of scientific inquiry. In order to formulate scientific laws, it is usually necessary to rule out factors which interfere with examining a specific causal relationship.

a. Capital outflow
b. Friedman-Savage utility function
c. Dematerialization
d. Ceteris paribus

Chapter 1. The Scope and Method of Economics

42. A _____ arises when one infers that something is true of the whole from the fact that it is true of some part of the whole (or even of every proper part.) For example: 'This fragment of metal cannot be broken with a hammer, therefore the machine of which it is a part cannot be broken with a hammer.' This is clearly fallacious, because many machines can be broken into their constituent parts without any of those parts being breakable.

This fallacy is often confused with the fallacy of hasty generalization, in which an unwarranted inference is made from a statement about a sample to a statement about the population from which it is drawn.

   a. Fallacy of composition
   b. 100-year flood
   c. 130-30 fund
   d. 1921 recession

43. _____, Latin for 'after this, therefore because of this', is a logical fallacy (of the questionable cause variety) which states, 'Since that event followed this one, that event must have been caused by this one.' It is often shortened to simply post hoc and is also sometimes referred to as false cause, coincidental correlation or correlation not causation. It is subtly different from the fallacy cum hoc ergo propter hoc, in which the chronological ordering of a correlation is insignificant.

Post hoc is a particularly tempting error because temporal sequence appears to be integral to causality.

   a. 100-year flood
   b. 130-30 fund
   c. 1921 recession
   d. Post hoc ergo propter hoc

44. _____ refers to the actions that governments take in the economic field. It covers the systems for setting interest rates and government deficit as well as the labour market, national ownership, and many other areas of government.

Such policies are often influenced by international institutions like the International Monetary Fund or World Bank as well as political beliefs and the consequent policies of parties.

   a. Economic policy
   b. AD-IA Model
   c. ACCRA Cost of Living Index
   d. ACEA agreement

45. _____ can be defined as the process of increasing economic integration between two countries, leading to the emergence of a global marketplace or a single world market. Depending on the paradigm, globalization can be viewed as both a positive and a negative phenomenon.

Whilst _____ has been occurring for the last several thousand years (since the emergence of trans-national trade), it has begun to occur at an increased rate over the last 20-30 years.

   a. Economic secession
   b. Autarchism
   c. Anarcho-capitalism
   d. Economic globalization

46. _____ is the concept or idea of fairness in economics, particularly as to taxation or welfare economics.

In welfare economics, _____ may be distinguished from economic efficiency in overall evaluation of social welfare. Although '_____' has broader uses, it may be posed as a counterpart to economic inequality in yielding a 'good' distribution of welfare.

Chapter 1. The Scope and Method of Economics

a. AD-IA Model
b. ACCRA Cost of Living Index
c. Equity
d. ACEA agreement

47. _____ in its literal sense is the process of transformation of local or regional phenomena into global ones. It can be described as a process by which the people of the world are unified into a single society and function together.

This process is a combination of economic, technological, sociocultural and political forces.

a. Globally Integrated Enterprise
b. Global Cosmopolitanism
c. Helsinki Process on Globalisation and Democracy
d. Globalization

48. _____ to the arrival of new individuals into a habitat or population. It is a biological concept and is important in population ecology, differentiated from emigration and migration.

_____ is a modern phenomenon.

a. ACCRA Cost of Living Index
b. AD-IA Model
c. ACEA agreement
d. Immigration

49. In statistics, signal processing, and many other fields, a _____ is a sequence of data points, measured typically at successive times, spaced at (often uniform) time intervals. _____ analysis comprises methods that attempt to understand such _____, often either to understand the underlying context of the data points (Where did they come from? What generated them?), or to make forecasts (predictions.) _____ forecasting is the use of a model to forecast future events based on known past events: to forecast future data points before they are measured.

a. Time series
b. Nonlinear regression
c. Heteroskedastic
d. First-hitting-time models

50. In mathematics, a _____ specifies each point uniquely in a plane by a pair of numerical coordinates, which are the signed distances from the point to two fixed perpendicular directed lines, measured in the same unit of length.

Each reference line is called a coordinate axis or just axis of the system, and the point where they meet is its origin. The coordinates can also be defined as the positions of the perpendicular projections of the point onto the two axes, expressed as a signed distances from the origin.

a. Cartesian coordinate system
b. 1921 recession
c. 130-30 fund
d. 100-year flood

51. _____ is a common concept in economics, and gives rise to derived concepts such as consumer debt. Generally _____ is defined by opposition to production. But the precise definition can vary because different schools of economists define production quite differently.

a. Cash or share options
b. Federal Reserve Bank Notes
c. Foreclosure data providers
d. Consumption

52. The _____ is 'the basic residential unit in which economic production, consumption, inheritance, child rearing, and shelter are organized and carried out'; [the _____] 'may or may not be synonymous with family'.

The _____ is the basic unit of analysis in many social, microeconomic and government models. The term refers to all individuals who live in the same dwelling.

a. 100-year flood
c. Household

b. Family economics
d. 130-30 fund

53. In coordinate geometry, the _____ is the y-value of the point where the graph of a function or relation intercepts the y-axis of the coordinate system.

In other words, the _____ of a function is the y-value of the point at which it intersects the line x = 0 (the y-axis.) Thus, if the function is specified in form y = f(x), the _____ is easy to find by calculating f.

a. 100-year flood
c. Ratio

b. 130-30 fund
d. Y-intercept

Chapter 2. The Economic Problem: Scarcity and Choice

1. _____s is the social science that studies the production, distribution, and consumption of goods and services. The term _____s comes from the Ancient Greek oá¼°κονομῖα from oá¼¶κος (oikos, 'house') + vÏŒμος (nomos, 'custom' or 'law'), hence 'rules of the house(hold)'. Current _____ models developed out of the broader field of political economy in the late 19th century, owing to a desire to use an empirical approach more akin to the physical sciences.
   a. Opportunity cost
   b. Energy economics
   c. Inflation
   d. Economic

2. _____ is a branch of economics that deals with the performance, structure, and behavior of a national or regional economy as a whole. Along with microeconomics, _____ is one of the two most general fields in economics. It is the study of the behavior and decision-making of entire economies.
   a. New Trade Theory
   b. Macroeconomics
   c. Tobit model
   d. Nominal value

3. _____ is a branch of economics that studies how individuals, households and firms and some states make decisions to allocate limited resources, typically in markets where goods or services are being bought and sold. _____ examines how these decisions and behaviours affect the supply and demand for goods and services, which determines prices; and how prices, in turn, determine the supply and demand of goods and services.

Whereas macroeconomics involves the 'sum total of economic activity, dealing with the issues of growth, inflation and unemployment, and with national economic policies relating to these issues' and the effects of government actions on them.

   a. Microeconomics
   b. Recession
   c. Countercyclical
   d. New Keynesian economics

4. In economics, _____ are the resources employed to produce goods and services. They facilitate production but do not become part of the product (as with raw materials) or significantly transformed by the production process (as with fuel used to power machinery.) To 19th century economists, the _____ were land (natural resources, gifts from nature), labor (the ability to work), and capital goods (human-made tools and equipment.)
   a. Long-run
   b. Hicks-neutral technical change
   c. Product Pipeline
   d. Factors of production

5. _____ is the term denoting either an entrance or changes which are inserted into a system and which activate/modify a process. It is an abstract concept, used in the modeling, system(s) design and system(s) exploitation. It is usually connected with other terms, e.g., _____ field, _____ variable, _____ parameter, _____ value, _____ signal, _____ device and _____ file.
   a. Input
   b. ACEA agreement
   c. AD-IA Model
   d. ACCRA Cost of Living Index

6. In microeconomics, _____ is quite simply the conversion of inputs into outputs. It is an economic process that uses resources to create a good or service that is suitable for exchange. This can include manufacturing, storing, shipping, and packaging.
   a. Solved
   b. Red Guards
   c. MET
   d. Production

Chapter 2. The Economic Problem: Scarcity and Choice

7. _____ or economic opportunity loss is the value of the next best alternative foregone as the result of making a decision. _____ analysis is an important part of a company's decision-making processes but is not treated as an actual cost in any financial statement. The next best thing that a person can engage in is referred to as the _____ of doing the best thing and ignoring the next best thing to be done.
- a. Economic ideology
- b. Economic
- c. Opportunity cost
- d. Industrial organization

8. In economics, _____ refers to the ability of a party to produce a good or service using fewer real resources than another entity producing the same good or service..A party has an _____ when using the same input as another party, it can produce a greater output. Since _____ is determined by a simple comparison of labor productivities, it is possible for a a party to have no _____ in anything. It can be contrasted with the concept of comparative advantage which refers to the ability to produce a particular good at a lower opportunity cost.
- a. Absolute advantage
- b. Index number
- c. ACCRA Cost of Living Index
- d. International economics

9. In economics, _____ refers to the ability of a person or a country to produce a particular good at a lower marginal cost and opportunity cost than another person or country. It is the ability to produce a product most efficiently given all the other products that could be produced. It can be contrasted with absolute advantage which refers to the ability of a person or a country to produce a particular good at a lower absolute cost than another.
- a. Hot money
- b. Gravity model of trade
- c. Triffin dilemma
- d. Comparative advantage

10. _____ measures the nominal future sum of money that a given sum of money is 'worth' at a specified time in the future assuming a certain interest rate rate of return; it is the present value multiplied by the accumulation function.

The value does not include corrections for inflation or other factors that affect the true value of money in the future. This is used in time value of money calculations.

- a. Negative gearing
- b. Present value
- c. Future-oriented
- d. Future value

11. _____ is the value on a given date of a future payment or series of future payments, discounted to reflect the time value of money and other factors such as investment risk. _____ calculations are widely used in business and economics to provide a means to compare cash flows at different times on a meaningful 'like to like' basis.

Money value fluctuates over time: $100 today are not worth $100 in five years.

- a. Future value
- b. Tax shield
- c. Present value of costs
- d. Present value

12. In economics, _____ is a measure of the relative satisfaction from consumption of various goods and services. Given this measure, one may speak meaningfully of increasing or decreasing _____, and thereby explain economic behavior in terms of attempts to increase one's _____. For illustrative purposes, changes in _____ are sometimes expressed in units called utils.

Chapter 2. The Economic Problem: Scarcity and Choice

a. Ordinal utility
c. Utility function

b. Utility
d. Expected utility hypothesis

13. In management accounting, _____ establishes budget and actual cost of operations, processes, departments or product and the analysis of variances, profitability or social use of funds. Managers use _____ to support decision-making to cut a company's costs and improve profitability. As a form of management accounting, _____ need not follow standards such as GAAP, because its primary use is for internal managers, rather than outside users, and what to compute is instead decided pragmatically.

a. Cost accounting
c. Khozraschyot

b. Total absorption costing
d. Quality costs

14. _____ is the a method of technical and economic research of the systems for purpose to optimize a parity between system's consumer functions or properties and expenses to achieve those functions or properties.

This methodology for continuous perfection of production, industrial technologies, organizational structures was developed by Juryj Sobolev in 1948 at the 'Perm telephone factory'

- 1948 Juryj Sobolev - the first success in application of a method analysis at the 'Perm telephone factory' .
- 1949 - the first application for the invention as result of use of the new method.

Today in economically developed countries practically each enterprise or the company use methodology of the kind of functional-cost analysis as a practice of the quality management, most full satisfying to principles of standards of series ISO 9000.

- Interest of consumer not in products itself, but the advantage which it will receive from its usage.
- The consumer aspires to reduce his expenses
- Functions needed by consumer can be executed in the various ways, and, hence, with various efficiency and expenses. Among possible alternatives of realization of functions exist such in which the parity of quality and the price is the optimal for the consumer.

The goal of _____ is achievement of the highest consumer satisfaction of production at simultaneous decrease in all kinds of industrial expenses Classical _____ has three English synonyms - Value Engineering, Value Management, Value Analysis.

a. Willingness to pay
c. Staple financing

b. Monopoly wage
d. Function cost analysis

15. In Marxian economics, _____ originally referred to the means of production. Individuals, organizations and governments use _____ in the production of other goods or commodities. _____ include factories, machinery, tools, equipment, and various buildings which are used to produce other products for consumption.

a. Capital goods
c. Wealth inequality in the United States

b. Capital intensive
d. Capital deepening

16. _____ is a broad label that refers to any individuals or households that use goods and services generated within the economy. The concept of a _____ is used in different contexts, so that the usage and significance of the term may vary.

Typically when business people and economists talk of _____s they are talking about person as _____, an aggregated commodity item with little individuality other than that expressed in the buy/not-buy decision.

a. 100-year flood
c. 130-30 fund
b. 1921 recession
d. Consumer

17. _____ are final goods specifically intended for the mass market. For instance, _____ do not include investment assets, like precious antiques, even though these antiques are final goods.

Manufactured goods are goods that have been processed by way of machinery.

a. Bulgarian-American trade
c. Fiscal stimulus plans
b. G-20 Leaders Summit on Financial Markets and the World Economy
d. Consumer goods

18. A _____ is an object whose consumption increases the utility of the consumer, for which the quantity demanded exceeds the quantity supplied at zero price. _____s are usually modeled as having diminishing marginal utility. The first individual purchase has high utility; the second has less.

a. Composite good
c. Pie method
b. Merit good
d. Good

19. The _____ was a worldwide economic downturn starting in most places in 1929 and ending at different times in the 1930s or early 1940s for different countries. It was the largest and most important economic depression in the 20th century, and is used in the 21st century as an example of how far the world's economy can fall. The _____ originated in the United States; historians most often use as a starting date the stock market crash on October 29, 1929, known as Black Tuesday.

a. Jarrow March
c. Wall Street Crash of 1929
b. British Empire Economic Conference
d. Great Depression

20. In economics, _____ refers to how the marginal contribution of a factor of production usually decreases as more of the factor is used. According to this relationship, in a production system with fixed and variable inputs, beyond some point, each additional unit of the variable input yields smaller and smaller increases in output. Conversely, producing one more unit of output costs more and more in variable inputs.

a. Diminishing returns
c. Derivatives law
b. Community property
d. Patent troll

21. In economics, the _____ is the rate at which a consumer is ready to give up one good in exchange for another good while maintaining the same level of satisfaction.

Under the standard assumption of neoclassical economics that goods and services are continuously divisible, the marginal rates of substitution will be the same regardless of the direction of exchange, and will correspond to the slope of an indifference curve (more precisely, to the slope multiplied by -1) passing through the consumption bundle in question, at that point: mathematically, it is the implicit derivative. MRS of Y for X is the amount of Y for which a consumer is willing to exchange for X locally.

a. Supply and demand
b. Marginal rate of substitution
c. Quality bias
d. Demand vacuum

22. In calculus, a function f defined on a subset of the real numbers with real values is called _____, if for all x and y such that x >≤ y one has f(x) >≤ f(y), so f preserves the order. In layman's terms, the sign of the slope is always positive (the curve tending upwards) or zero (i.e., non-decreasing, or asymptotic, or depicted as a horizontal, flat line) Likewise, a function is called monotonically decreasing (non-increasing) if, whenever x >≤ y, then f(x) >≥ f(y), so it reverses the order.

a. 130-30 fund
b. 100-year flood
c. 1921 recession
d. Monotonic

23. _____ can be defined as the process of increasing economic integration between two countries, leading to the emergence of a global marketplace or a single world market. Depending on the paradigm, globalization can be viewed as both a positive and a negative phenomenon.

Whilst _____ has been occurring for the last several thousand years (since the emergence of trans-national trade), it has begun to occur at an increased rate over the last 20-30 years.

a. Anarcho-capitalism
b. Economic secession
c. Autarchism
d. Economic globalization

24. _____ is the increase in the amount of the goods and services produced by an economy over time. It is conventionally measured as the percent rate of increase in real gross domestic product, or real GDP. Growth is usually calculated in real terms, i.e. inflation-adjusted terms, in order to net out the effect of inflation on the price of the goods and services produced.

a. ACEA agreement
b. ACCRA Cost of Living Index
c. AD-IA Model
d. Economic growth

25. _____ in its literal sense is the process of transformation of local or regional phenomena into global ones. It can be described as a process by which the people of the world are unified into a single society and function together.

This process is a combination of economic, technological, sociocultural and political forces.

a. Globalization
b. Helsinki Process on Globalisation and Democracy
c. Globally Integrated Enterprise
d. Global Cosmopolitanism

26. _____ in economics refers to metrics and measures of output from production processes, per unit of input. Labor _____, for example, is typically measured as a ratio of output per labor-hour, an input. _____ may be conceived of as a metrics of the technical or engineering efficiency of production.

a. Fordism
b. Production-possibility frontier
c. Piece work
d. Productivity

27. The _____, sometimes called the fundamental _____, is one of the fundamental economic theories in the operation of any economy. It asserts that there is scarcity, that the finite resources available are insufficient to satisfy all human wants. The problem then becomes how to determine what is to be produced and how the factors of production (such as capital and labour) are to be allocated.
   a. Economic nationalism
   b. Economic problem
   c. Eclectic paradigm
   d. Endogenous growth theory

28. An _____ or Å"conomic system is a system that involves the production, distribution and consumption of goods and services between the entities in a particular society. It is the method used by society to produce and distribute goods and services. The _____ is composed of people and institutions, including their relationships to productive resources, such as through the convention of property.
   a. Intention economy
   b. Economic system
   c. Information economy
   d. Indicative planning

29. _____ is a term used to describe a policy of allowing events to take their own course. The term is a French phrase literally meaning 'let do'. It is a doctrine that states that government generally should not intervene in the marketplace.
   a. Theory of Productive Forces
   b. Communization
   c. Laissez-faire
   d. Heroic capitalism

30. _____ is a term which is used in economics to refer to the rule or sovereignty of purchasers in markets as to production of goods. It is the power of consumers to decide what gets produced. People use the this term to describe the consumer as the 'king,' or ruler, of the market, the one who determines what products will be produced.
   a. Schedule delay
   b. Consumer sovereignty
   c. Reservation price
   d. Microeconomic reform

31. A _____ is a theoretical term that economists use to describe a market which is free from government intervention (i.e. no regulation, no subsidization, no single monetary system and no governmental monopolies.) In a _____, property rights are voluntarily exchanged at a price arranged solely by the mutual consent of sellers and buyers. By definition, buyers and sellers do not coerce each other, in the sense that they obtain each other's property without the use of physical force, threat of physical force, or fraud, nor is the coerced by a third party (such as by government via transfer payments) and they engage in trade simply because they both consent and believe that it is a good enough choice.
   a. Third camp
   b. Leninism
   c. Delegation
   d. Free market

32. In business, _____ is the total liabilitiess minus total outside assets of an individual or a company. For a company, this is called shareholders' prefernce and may be referred to as book value. _____ is stated as at a particular year in time.
   a. Net worth
   b. Bond credit rating
   c. Sinking fund
   d. Post earnings announcement drift

33. _____ in economics and business is the result of an exchange and from that trade we assign a numerical monetary value to a good, service or asset. If Alice trades Bob 4 apples for an orange, the _____ of an orange is 4 apples. Inversely, the _____ of an apple is 1/4 oranges.

a. Premium pricing b. Price war
c. Price book d. Price

34. Applied microeconomics includes a range of specialized areas of study, many of which draw on methods from other fields. Applied work often uses little more than the basics of _____, supply and demand. Industrial organization and regulation examines topics such as the entry and exit of firms, innovation, role of trademarks.

a. Microeconomics b. Monopolistic competition
c. Financial crises d. Price theory

35. The _____ is 'the basic residential unit in which economic production, consumption, inheritance, child rearing, and shelter are organized and carried out'; [the _____] 'may or may not be synonymous with family'.

The _____ is the basic unit of analysis in many social, microeconomic and government models. The term refers to all individuals who live in the same dwelling.

a. Family economics b. Household
c. 100-year flood d. 130-30 fund

36. A _____ is an economy based on the division of labor in which the prices of goods and services are determined in a free price system set by supply and demand. This is often contrasted with a planned economy, in which a central government determines the price of goods and services using a fixed price system. Market economies are contrasted with mixed economy where the price system is not entirely free but under some government control that is not extensive enough to constitute a planned economy.

a. Network Economy b. Commons-based peer production
c. Market economy d. Nutritional Economics

37. To _____ is to impose a financial charge or other levy upon a taxpayer by a state or the functional equivalent of a state.

_____es are also imposed by many subnational entities. _____es consist of direct _____ or indirect _____, and may be paid in money or as its labour equivalent (often but not always unpaid.)

a. 130-30 fund b. Tax
c. 1921 recession d. 100-year flood

38. A _____ is an economic system that incorporates a mixture of private and government ownership or control, or a mixture of capitalism and socialism.

There is not one single definition for a _____, but relevant aspects include: a degree of private economic freedom (including privately owned industry) intermingled with centralized economic planning and government regulation (which may include regulation of the market for environmental concerns and social welfare, or state ownership and management of some of the means of production for national or social objectives.)

For some states, there is not a consensus on whether they are capitalist, socialist, or mixed economies.

Chapter 2. The Economic Problem: Scarcity and Choice

a. Planned liberalism
c. Dual economy
b. Hunter-gatherer
d. Mixed economy

39. An _____ is a person who has possession of an enterprise and assumes significant accountability for the inherent risks and the outcome. It is an ambitious leader who combines land, labor, and capital to create and market new goods or services. The term is a loanword from French and was first defined by the Irish economist Richard Cantillon.

a. Expansionary policies
c. ACEA agreement
b. ACCRA Cost of Living Index
d. Entrepreneur

40. In economics, _____ is the active redirecting resources from being consumed today so that they may create benefits in the future; the use of assets to earn income or profit._____ is the process of making an investment in order to earn a profit, for example equity investment either through a fund, a 401k plan, or individually. People often invest in order to build up their estate or to accumulate funds for retirement.

To try to predict good stocks to invest in, two main schools of thought exist: technical analysis and fundamentals analysis.

a. ACCRA Cost of Living Index
c. Investing
b. ACEA agreement
d. AD-IA Model

Chapter 3. Demand, Supply, and Market Equilibrium

1. The _____ is 'the basic residential unit in which economic production, consumption, inheritance, child rearing, and shelter are organized and carried out'; [the _____] 'may or may not be synonomous with family'.

The _____ is the basic unit of analysis in many social, microeconomic and government models. The term refers to all individuals who live in the same dwelling.

   a. 100-year flood
   b. Family economics
   c. 130-30 fund
   d. Household

2. An _____ is a person who has possession of an enterprise and assumes significant accountability for the inherent risks and the outcome. It is an ambitious leader who combines land, labor, and capital to create and market new goods or services. The term is a loanword from French and was first defined by the Irish economist Richard Cantillon.
   a. ACCRA Cost of Living Index
   b. ACEA agreement
   c. Entrepreneur
   d. Expansionary policies

3. _____ is the term denoting either an entrance or changes which are inserted into a system and which activate/modify a process. It is an abstract concept, used in the modeling, system(s) design and system(s) exploitation. It is usually connected with other terms, e.g., _____ field, _____ variable, _____ parameter, _____ value, _____ signal, _____ device and _____ file.
   a. ACCRA Cost of Living Index
   b. ACEA agreement
   c. AD-IA Model
   d. Input

4. The _____ is the market for securities, where companies and governments can raise longterm funds. It is a market in which money is lent for periods longer than a year. The _____ includes the stock market and the bond market.
   a. Multi-family office
   b. Capital market
   c. Performance attribution
   d. Financial instrument

5. In economics, the term _____ of income or _____ refers to a simple economic model which describes the reciprocal circulation of income between producers and consumers. In the _____ model, the inter-dependent entities of producer and consumer are referred to as 'firms' and 'households' respectively and provide each other with factors in order to facilitate the flow of income. Firms provide consumers with goods and services in exchange for consumer expenditure and 'factors of production' from households.
   a. 100-year flood
   b. 1921 recession
   c. 130-30 fund
   d. Circular flow

6. In economics, _____ are the resources employed to produce goods and services. They facilitate production but do not become part of the product (as with raw materials) or significantly transformed by the production process (as with fuel used to power machinery.) To 19th century economists, the _____ were land (natural resources, gifts from nature), labor (the ability to work), and capital goods (human-made tools and equipment.)
   a. Product Pipeline
   b. Long-run
   c. Factors of production
   d. Hicks-neutral technical change

7. _____s is the social science that studies the production, distribution, and consumption of goods and services. The term _____s comes from the Ancient Greek οἰκονομῐ́α from οἶκος (oikos, 'house') + νόμος (nomos, 'custom' or 'law'), hence 'rules of the house(hold)'. Current _____ models developed out of the broader field of political economy in the late 19th century, owing to a desire to use an empirical approach more akin to the physical sciences.

Chapter 3. Demand, Supply, and Market Equilibrium

a. Opportunity cost
b. Energy economics
c. Inflation
d. Economic

8. In microeconomics, _____ is quite simply the conversion of inputs into outputs. It is an economic process that uses resources to create a good or service that is suitable for exchange. This can include manufacturing, storing, shipping, and packaging.

a. Solved
b. Production
c. MET
d. Red Guards

9. CÄ"terÄ«s paribus is a Latin phrase, literally translated as 'with other things the same.' It is commonly rendered in English as 'all other things being equal.' A prediction, or a statement about causal or logical connections between two states of affairs, is qualified by _____ in order to acknowledge, and to rule out, the possibility of other factors which could override the relationship between the antecedent and the consequent.

A _____ assumption is often fundamental to the predictive purpose of scientific inquiry. In order to formulate scientific laws, it is usually necessary to rule out factors which interfere with examining a specific causal relationship.

a. Capital outflow
b. Dematerialization
c. Friedman-Savage utility function
d. Ceteris paribus

10. _____ is an economic model based on price, utility and quantity in a market. It predicts that in a competitive market, price will function to equalize the quantity demanded by consumers, and the quantity supplied by producers, resulting in an economic equilibrium of price and quantity. The model incorporates other factors changing equilibrium as a shift of demand and/or supply.

a. Joint demand
b. Deferred gratification
c. Rational addiction
d. Supply and demand

11. Economics:

- _____ ,the desire to own something and the ability to pay for it
- _____ curve,a graphic representation of a _____ schedule
- _____ deposit, the money in checking accounts
- _____ pull theory,the theory that inflation occurs when _____ for goods and services exceeds existing supplies
- _____ schedule,a table that lists the quantity of a good a person will buy it each different price
- _____ side economics,the school of economics at believes government spending and tax cuts open economy by raising _____

a. McKesson ' Robbins scandal
b. Demand
c. Variability
d. Production

12. _____ is a mechanism that allows people easily to buy and sell products. Services are often included in the scope of the term. _____ regulation is an economic term that describes restrictions in the market.

Chapter 3. Demand, Supply, and Market Equilibrium

    a. Market dominance   b. Financialization
    c. Fixed exchange rate system   d. Product market

13. In economics, the _____ can be defined as the graph depicting the relationship between the price of a certain commodity, and the amount of it that consumers are willing and able to purchase at that given price. It is a graphic representation of a demand schedule. The _____ for all consumers together follows from the _____ of every individual consumer: the individual demands at each price are added together.
    a. Cost curve   b. Kuznets curve
    c. Demand curve   d. Wage curve

14. In economics, a _____ is a table that lists the quantity of a good a person will buy it each different price See Demand curve.
    a. Rational irrationality   b. Free contract
    c. Federal Reserve districts   d. Demand schedule

15. In economics, the _____ is an economic law that states that consumers buy more of a good when its price decreases and less when its price increases.

There are certain goods which do not follow this law. These include Veblen and Giffen goods

    a. Georgism   b. Market failure
    c. Financial crisis   d. Law of demand

16. In economics, _____ is a measure of the relative satisfaction from consumption of various goods and services. Given this measure, one may speak meaningfully of increasing or decreasing _____, and thereby explain economic behavior in terms of attempts to increase one's _____. For illustrative purposes, changes in _____ are sometimes expressed in units called utils.
    a. Expected utility hypothesis   b. Ordinal utility
    c. Utility function   d. Utility

17. In economics, the _____ of a good or of a service is the utility of the specific use to which an agent would put a given increase in that good or service, or of the specific use that would be abandoned in response to a given decrease. In other words, _____ is the utility of the marginal use -- which, on the assumption of economic rationality, would be the least urgent use of the good or service, from the best feasible combination of actions in which its use is included. Under the mainstream assumptions, the _____ of a good or service is the posited quantified change in utility obtained by increasing or by decreasing use of that good or service.
    a. Marginal utility   b. 100-year flood
    c. 130-30 fund   d. 1921 recession

18. In algebra, a _____ is a function depending on n that associates a scalar, det(A), to an n×n square matrix A. The fundamental geometric meaning of a _____ is a scale factor for measure when A is regarded as a linear transformation. _____s are important both in calculus, where they enter the substitution rule for several variables, and in multilinear algebra.

For a fixed nonnegative integer n, there is a unique _____ function for the n×n matrices over any commutative ring R. In particular, this function exists when R is the field of real or complex numbers.

Chapter 3. Demand, Supply, and Market Equilibrium

a. 1921 recession
b. 130-30 fund
c. 100-year flood
d. Determinant

19. To _____ is to impose a financial charge or other levy upon a taxpayer by a state or the functional equivalent of a state.

_____es are also imposed by many subnational entities. _____es consist of direct _____ or indirect _____, and may be paid in money or as its labour equivalent (often but not always unpaid.)

a. Tax
b. 1921 recession
c. 100-year flood
d. 130-30 fund

20. A _____ or complement good in economics is a good which is consumed with another good; its cross elasticity of demand is negative. - It is two goods that are bought and used together. This means that, if goods A and B were complements, more of good A being bought would result in more of good B also being bought.

a. Manufactured goods
b. Free good
c. Final good
d. Complementary good

21. A _____ is an object whose consumption increases the utility of the consumer, for which the quantity demanded exceeds the quantity supplied at zero price. _____s are usually modeled as having diminishing marginal utility. The first individual purchase has high utility; the second has less.

a. Merit good
b. Pie method
c. Good
d. Composite good

22. In consumer theory, an _____ is a good that decreases in demand when consumer income rises, unlike normal goods, for which the opposite is observed. It is a good that consumers demand increases when their income increases. Inferiority, in this sense, is an observable fact relating to affordability rather than a statement about the quality of the good.

a. Information good
b. Independent goods
c. Export-oriented
d. Inferior good

23. In business, _____ is the total liabilitiess minus total outside assets of an individual or a company. For a company, this is called shareholders' prefernce and may be referred to as book value. _____ is stated as at a particular year in time.

a. Post earnings announcement drift
b. Bond credit rating
c. Net worth
d. Sinking fund

24. In economics, _____s are any goods for which demand increases when income increases and falls when income decreases but price remains constant, i.e. with a positive income elasticity of demand. The term does not necessarily refer to the quality of the good.

Depending on the indifference curves, the amount of a good bought can either increase, decrease, or stay the same when income increases.

a. Normative economics
b. Financial contagion
c. Bord halfpenny
d. Normal good

Chapter 3. Demand, Supply, and Market Equilibrium

25. In economics, the _____ is the tendency of suppliers to offer more of a good at a higher price. The relationship between price and quantity supplied is usually a positive relationship. A rise in price is associated with a rise in quantity supplied.
    a. Mathematical economics
    b. Market failure
    c. Law of supply
    d. Heterodox economics

26. _____ in economics and business is the result of an exchange and from that trade we assign a numerical monetary value to a good, service or asset. If Alice trades Bob 4 apples for an orange, the _____ of an orange is 4 apples. Inversely, the _____ of an apple is 1/4 oranges.
    a. Price war
    b. Price book
    c. Premium pricing
    d. Price

27. A _____ is a theoretical term that economists use to describe a market which is free from government intervention (i.e. no regulation, no subsidization, no single monetary system and no governmental monopolies.) In a _____, property rights are voluntarily exchanged at a price arranged solely by the mutual consent of sellers and buyers. By definition, buyers and sellers do not coerce each other, in the sense that they obtain each other's property without the use of physical force, threat of physical force, or fraud, nor is the coerced by a third party (such as by government via transfer payments) and they engage in trade simply because they both consent and believe that it is a good enough choice.
    a. Leninism
    b. Delegation
    c. Third camp
    d. Free market

28. _____ or economic opportunity loss is the value of the next best alternative foregone as the result of making a decision. _____ analysis is an important part of a company's decision-making processes but is not treated as an actual cost in any financial statement. The next best thing that a person can engage in is referred to as the _____ of doing the best thing and ignoring the next best thing to be done.
    a. Economic
    b. Economic ideology
    c. Opportunity cost
    d. Industrial organization

29. _____ is a term that is used to describe the overall process of invention, innovation and diffusion of technology or processes. The term is redundant with technological development, technological achievement, and technological progress. In essence _____ is the invention of a technology (or a process), the continuous process of improving a technology (in which it often becomes cheaper) and its diffusion throughout industry or society.
    a. 1921 recession
    b. 100-year flood
    c. 130-30 fund
    d. Technological change

30. In management accounting, _____ establishes budget and actual cost of operations, processes, departments or product and the analysis of variances, profitability or social use of funds. Managers use _____ to support decision-making to cut a company's costs and improve profitability. As a form of management accounting, _____ need not follow standards such as GAAP, because its primary use is for internal managers, rather than outside users, and what to compute is instead decided pragmatically.
    a. Quality costs
    b. Khozraschyot
    c. Total absorption costing
    d. Cost accounting

31. In economics, _____ is when quantity demanded is more than quantity supplied.See Economic shortage.

a. Excess demand
c. ACEA agreement
b. AD-IA Model
d. ACCRA Cost of Living Index

32. In economics, economic equilibrium is simply a state of the world where economic forces are balanced and in the absence of external influences the (equilibrium) values of economic variables will not change. It is the point at which quantity demanded and quantity supplied are equal. _____, for example, refers to a condition where a market price is established through competition such that the amount of goods or services sought by buyers is equal to the amount of goods or services produced by sellers.
   a. Market equilibrium
   c. Marketization
   b. Product-Market Growth Matrix
   d. Regulated market

33. _____ is the controlled distribution of resources and scarce goods or services. _____ controls the size of the ration, one's allotted portion of the resources being distributed on a particular day or at a particular time.

In economics, it is often common to use the word '_____' to refer to one of the roles that prices play in markets, while _____ is called 'non-price _____.' Using prices to ration means that those with the most money (or other assets) and who want a product the most are first to receive it.

   a. Rationing
   c. 1921 recession
   b. 100-year flood
   d. 130-30 fund

34. _____ is the application of economic techniques to real estate markets. It tries to describe, explain, and predict patterns of prices, supply, and demand. The closely related fields of housing economics is narrower in scope, concentrating on residential real estate markets as does the research of real estate trends focus on the business and structural changes impacting the industry.
   a. 100-year flood
   c. 1921 recession
   b. Real estate economics
   d. 130-30 fund

35. In economics, _____ is when quantity supplied is more than quantity demanded. .
   a. Effective unemployment rate
   c. Economic Value Creation
   b. Illicit financial flows
   d. Excess supply

36. _____ or market division schemes are agreements in which competitors divide markets among themselves. In such schemes, competing firms allocate specific customers or types of customers, products, or territories among themselves. For example, one competitor will be allowed to sell to, or bid on contracts let by, certain customers or types of customers.
   a. G-20 Leaders Summit on Financial Markets and the World Economy
   c. History of minimum wage
   b. Discrete choice
   d. Market allocation

37. _____ is used to assign the available resources in an economic way. It is part of resource management.

In strategic planning,is a plan for using available resources, for example human resources, especially in the near term, to achieve goals for the future.

a. 100-year flood
b. 130-30 fund
c. 1921 recession
d. Resource allocation

38. A _____ is something for which there is demand, but which is supplied without qualitative differentiation across a market. It is a product that is the same no matter who produces it, such as petroleum, notebook paper, or milk. In other words, copper is copper.
   a. 100-year flood
   b. Commodity
   c. Hard commodity
   d. Soft commodity

39. _____ was a survey conducted by the U.S. Department of Justice to gauge the prevalence of alcohol and illegal drug use among prior arrestees. It was a reformulation of the prior Drug Use Forecasting (DUF) program, focused on five drugs in particular: cocaine, marijuana, methamphetamine, opiates, and PCP.

Participants were randomly selected from arrest records in major metropolitan areas; because no personally identifying information is taken from each record chosen, the resulting data can be correlated to arrest rates, but not to the total population of persons charged.

   a. AD-IA Model
   b. ACCRA Cost of Living Index
   c. Arrestee Drug Abuse Monitoring
   d. ACEA agreement

40. In economics, the _____ is the term economists use to describe the self-regulating nature of the marketplace. The _____ is a metaphor coined by the economist Adam Smith in The Wealth of Nations.

Adam Smith mentions the metaphor in Book IV of The Wealth of Nations, arguing that people in any society will certainly employ their capital in foreign trading only if the profits available by that method far exceed those available locally, and that in such a case it is better for society as a whole if they so did.

   a. AD-IA Model
   b. ACCRA Cost of Living Index
   c. Invisible hand
   d. ACEA agreement

41. _____ was a Scottish moral philosopher and a pioneer of political economy. One of the key figures of the Scottish Enlightenment, Smith is the author of The Theory of Moral Sentiments and An Inquiry into the Nature and Causes of the Wealth of Nations. The latter, usually abbreviated as The Wealth of Nations, is considered his magnum opus and the first modern work of economics.
   a. Adolph Fischer
   b. Adolf Hitler
   c. Alan Greenspan
   d. Adam Smith

Chapter 4. Demand and Supply Applications and Elasticity

1. In economics, economic equilibrium is simply a state of the world where economic forces are balanced and in the absence of external influences the (equilibrium) values of economic variables will not change. It is the point at which quantity demanded and quantity supplied are equal. _____, for example, refers to a condition where a market price is established through competition such that the amount of goods or services sought by buyers is equal to the amount of goods or services produced by sellers.
   - a. Regulated market
   - b. Product-Market Growth Matrix
   - c. Marketization
   - d. Market equilibrium

2. _____ in economics and business is the result of an exchange and from that trade we assign a numerical monetary value to a good, service or asset. If Alice trades Bob 4 apples for an orange, the _____ of an orange is 4 apples. Inversely, the _____ of an apple is 1/4 oranges.
   - a. Price war
   - b. Price book
   - c. Premium pricing
   - d. Price

3. In economics, a _____ is any economic system that effects its distribution of goods and services with prices and employing any form of money or debt tokens. Except for possible remote and primitive communities, all modern societies use _____s to allocate resources. However, _____s are not used for all resource allocation decisions today.
   - a. Hanseatic League
   - b. Neomercantilism
   - c. Price system
   - d. Family economy

4. _____ is the controlled distribution of resources and scarce goods or services. _____ controls the size of the ration, one's allotted portion of the resources being distributed on a particular day or at a particular time.

   In economics, it is often common to use the word '_____' to refer to one of the roles that prices play in markets, while _____ is called 'non-price _____.' Using prices to ration means that those with the most money (or other assets) and who want a product the most are first to receive it.
   - a. 1921 recession
   - b. 130-30 fund
   - c. 100-year flood
   - d. Rationing

5. A _____ is a theoretical term that economists use to describe a market which is free from government intervention (i.e. no regulation, no subsidization, no single monetary system and no governmental monopolies.) In a _____, property rights are voluntarily exchanged at a price arranged solely by the mutual consent of sellers and buyers. By definition, buyers and sellers do not coerce each other, in the sense that they obtain each other's property without the use of physical force, threat of physical force, or fraud, nor is the coerced by a third party (such as by government via transfer payments) and they engage in trade simply because they both consent and believe that it is a good enough choice.
   - a. Free market
   - b. Leninism
   - c. Third camp
   - d. Delegation

6. In economics, the _____ is the maximum amount a person would be willing to pay, sacrifice or exchange for a good.

   Choice modelling techniques may be used to estimate the value of the _____ through a choice experiment.
   - a. Global strategy
   - b. Willingness to pay
   - c. Net pay
   - d. Round-tripping

7. The Organization of the Petroleum Exporting Countries is a cartel of twelve countries made up of Algeria, Angola, Ecuador, Iran, Iraq, Kuwait, Libya, Nigeria, Qatar, Saudi Arabia, the United Arab Emirates, and Venezuela. The cartel has maintained its headquarters in Vienna since 1965, and hosts regular meetings among the oil ministers of its Member Countries. Indonesia withdrew its membership in _____ in 2008 after it became a net importer of oil, but stated it would likely return if it became a net exporter in the world.
   a. OPEC
   b. ACCRA Cost of Living Index
   c. AD-IA Model
   d. ACEA agreement

8. In international commerce and politics, an _____ is the prohibition of commerce (division of trade) and trade with a certain country, in order to isolate it and to put its government into a difficult internal situation, given that the effects of the _____ are often able to make its economy suffer from the initiative.

   The _____ is usually used as a political punishment for some previous disagreed policies or acts, but its economic nature frequently raises doubts about the real interests that the prohibition serves.

   One of the most comprehensive attempts at an _____ happened during the Napoleonic Wars.

   a. International finance
   b. Overshooting model
   c. Embargo
   d. Optimum currency area

9. A _____ is a government imposed limit on how high a price can be charged on a product. For a _____ to be effective, it must differ from the free market price. In the graph at right, the supply and demand curves intersect to determine the free-market quantity and price.
   a. Fire sale
   b. Pricing
   c. Product sabotage
   d. Price ceiling

10. The underground economy or _____ is a market where all commerce is conducted without regard to taxation, law or regulations of trade. The term is also often known as the underdog, shadow economy, black economy, parallel economy or phantom trades.

    In modern societies the underground economy covers a vast array of activities.

    a. Black market
    b. Social market economy
    c. Protectionism
    d. Market economy

11. In microeconomics, _____ is quite simply the conversion of inputs into outputs. It is an economic process that uses resources to create a good or service that is suitable for exchange. This can include manufacturing, storing, shipping, and packaging.
    a. Red Guards
    b. Solved
    c. MET
    d. Production

12. _____ is used to assign the available resources in an economic way. It is part of resource management.

    In strategic planning, is a plan for using available resources, for example human resources, especially in the near term, to achieve goals for the future.

a. 1921 recession
c. Resource allocation
b. 100-year flood
d. 130-30 fund

13. Economics:

- _____, the desire to own something and the ability to pay for it
- _____ curve, a graphic representation of a _____ schedule
- _____ deposit, the money in checking accounts
- _____ pull theory, the theory that inflation occurs when _____ for goods and services exceeds existing supplies
- _____ schedule, a table that lists the quantity of a good a person will buy it each different price
- _____ side economics, the school of economics at believes government spending and tax cuts open economy by raising _____

a. Demand
c. Production
b. McKesson ' Robbins scandal
d. Variability

14. A _____ is the lowest hourly, daily or monthly wage that employers may legally pay to employees or workers. Equivalently, it is the lowest wage at which workers may sell their labor. Although _____ laws are in effect in a great many jurisdictions, there are differences of opinion about the benefits and drawbacks of a _____.

a. Permanent war economy
c. Microfoundations
b. Marginal propensity to consume
d. Minimum wage

15. A _____ is a government- or group-imposed limit on how low a price can be charged for a product. In order for a _____ to be effective, it must be greater than the equilibrium price. An ineffective _____, below equilibrium price.

A _____ can be set below the free-market equilibrium price.

a. Two-part tariff
c. Flat rate
b. Price markdown
d. Price floor

16. _____ is an economic model based on price, utility and quantity in a market. It predicts that in a competitive market, price will function to equalize the quantity demanded by consumers, and the quantity supplied by producers, resulting in an economic equilibrium of price and quantity. The model incorporates other factors changing equilibrium as a shift of demand and/or supply.

a. Joint demand
c. Supply and demand
b. Rational addiction
d. Deferred gratification

17. Under the system of feudalism, a _____, fief, feud, feoff often consisted of inheritable lands or revenue-producing property granted by a liege lord, generally to a vassal, in return for a form of allegiance, originally to give him the means to fulfill his military duties when called upon. However anything of value could be held in fief, such as an office, a right of exploitation (e.g., hunting, fishing) or any other type of revenue, rather than the land it comes from.

Originally, the feudal institution of vassalage did not imply the giving or receiving of landholdings (which were granted only as a reward for loyalty), but by the eighth century the giving of a landholding was becoming standard.

    a. 1921 recession
    b. 100-year flood
    c. 130-30 fund
    d. Fiefdom

18. In economics, an _____ is any good (e.g. a commodity) or service brought into one country from another country in a legitimate fashion, typically for use in trade.It is a good that is brought in from another country for sale. _____ goods or services are provided to domestic consumers by foreign producers. An _____ in the receiving country is an export to the sending country.
    a. Incoterms
    b. Import quota
    c. Economic integration
    d. Import

19. _____ is a broad label that refers to any individuals or households that use goods and services generated within the economy. The concept of a _____ is used in different contexts, so that the usage and significance of the term may vary.

Typically when business people and economists talk of _____s they are talking about person as _____, an aggregated commodity item with little individuality other than that expressed in the buy/not-buy decision.

    a. 100-year flood
    b. 1921 recession
    c. Consumer
    d. 130-30 fund

20. The term surplus is used in economics for several related quantities. The _____ is the amount that consumers benefit by being able to purchase a product for a price that is less than they would be willing to pay. The producer surplus is the amount that producers benefit by selling at a market price mechanism that is higher than they would be willing to sell for.
    a. Necessity good
    b. Microeconomic reform
    c. Marginal rate of technical substitution
    d. Consumer surplus

21. The term surplus is used in economics for several related quantities. The consumer surplus is the amount that consumers benefit by being able to purchase a product for a price that is less than they would be willing to pay. The _____ is the amount that producers benefit by selling at a market price mechanism that is higher than they would be willing to sell for.
    a. Returns to scale
    b. Long term
    c. Schedule delay
    d. Producer surplus

22. In economics, a _____ is a loss of economic efficiency that can occur when equilibrium for a good or service is not Pareto optimal. In other words, either people who would have more marginal benefit than marginal cost are not buying the good or service, or people who would have more marginal cost than marginal benefit are buying the product.

Causes of _____ can include monopoly pricing, externalities, taxes or subsidies, and binding price ceilings or floors.

a. Deadweight loss
b. Distributive efficiency
c. Leapfrogging
d. Contract curve

23. In economics, _____ refers to excess of supply over demand of products being offered to the market. This leads to lower prices and/or unsold goods.

_____ is the accumulation of unsalable inventories in the hands of businesses.

a. Incomplete markets
b. Inflation adjustment
c. Intra Regional Trade
d. Overproduction

24. Necessary _____ s:

If x is a necessary _____ of y, then the presence of y necessarily implies the presence of x. The presence of x, however, does not imply that y will occur.

Sufficient _____ s:

If x is a sufficient _____ of y, then the presence of x necessarily implies the presence of y.

a. Philosophy of economics
b. Political philosophy
c. Cause
d. Materialism

25. CÄ"terÄ«s paribus is a Latin phrase, literally translated as 'with other things the same.' It is commonly rendered in English as 'all other things being equal.' A prediction, or a statement about causal or logical connections between two states of affairs, is qualified by _____ in order to acknowledge, and to rule out, the possibility of other factors which could override the relationship between the antecedent and the consequent.

A _____ assumption is often fundamental to the predictive purpose of scientific inquiry. In order to formulate scientific laws, it is usually necessary to rule out factors which interfere with examining a specific causal relationship.

a. Ceteris paribus
b. Friedman-Savage utility function
c. Capital outflow
d. Dematerialization

26. In economics, the _____ can be defined as the graph depicting the relationship between the price of a certain commodity, and the amount of it that consumers are willing and able to purchase at that given price. It is a graphic representation of a demand schedule. The _____ for all consumers together follows from the _____ of every individual consumer: the individual demands at each price are added together.

a. Cost curve
b. Wage curve
c. Demand curve
d. Kuznets curve

27. _____ is defined as the measure of responsiveness in the quantity demanded for a commodity as a result of change in price of the same commodity. It is a measure of how consumers react to a change in price. In other words, it is percentage change in quantity demanded as per the percentage change in price of the same commodity.

Chapter 4. Demand and Supply Applications and Elasticity

a. 100-year flood
b. 1921 recession
c. Price elasticity of demand
d. 130-30 fund

28. In economics, _____ is the ratio of the percent change in one variable to the percent change in another variable. It is a tool for measuring the responsiveness of a function to changes in parameters in a relative way. Commonly analyzed are _____ of substitution, price and wealth.
 a. ACEA agreement
 b. Elasticity
 c. ACCRA Cost of Living Index
 d. Elasticity of demand

29. Price _____ is defined as the measure of responsiveness in the quantity demanded for a commodity as a result of change in price of the same commodity. It is a measure of how consumers react to a change in price. In other words, it is percentage change in quantity demanded by the percentage change in price of the same commodity.
 a. ACEA agreement
 b. Elasticity of Demand
 c. Elasticity
 d. ACCRA Cost of Living Index

30. In economics, _____ describes demand that is not very sensitive to a change in price.
 a. Effective unemployment rate
 b. Export-led growth
 c. Inelastic
 d. Inflation hedge

31. A _____ is an expression that compares quantities relative to each other. The most common examples involve two quantities, but any number of quantities can be compared. _____s are represented mathematically by separating each quantity with a colon, for example the _____ 2:3, which is read as the _____ 'two to three'.
 a. 130-30 fund
 b. 100-year flood
 c. Y-intercept
 d. Ratio

32. _____ is the total money received from the sale of any given quantity of output.

The _____ is calculated by taking the price of the sale times the quantity sold, i.e.

_____ = price X quantity.

 a. Market development funds
 b. Ceteris paribus
 c. Total revenue
 d. Small numbers game

33. In algebra, a _____ is a function depending on n that associates a scalar, det(A), to an n×n square matrix A. The fundamental geometric meaning of a _____ is a scale factor for measure when A is regarded as a linear transformation. _____s are important both in calculus, where they enter the substitution rule for several variables, and in multilinear algebra.

For a fixed nonnegative integer n, there is a unique _____ function for the n×n matrices over any commutative ring R. In particular, this function exists when R is the field of real or complex numbers.

 a. 130-30 fund
 b. 1921 recession
 c. 100-year flood
 d. Determinant

Chapter 4. Demand and Supply Applications and Elasticity

34. In economics, the _____ of demand measures the responsiveness of the demand of a good to the change in the income of the people demanding the good. It is calculated as the ratio of the percent change in demand to the percent change in income. For example, if, in response to a 10% increase in income, the demand of a good increased by 20%, the _____ of demand would be 20%/10% = 2.
    a. ACCRA Cost of Living Index
    b. ACEA agreement
    c. Income elasticity
    d. AD-IA Model

35. In economics, the _____ measures the responsiveness of the demand of a good to the change in the income of the people demanding the good. It is calculated as the ratio of the percent change in demand to the percent change in income. For example, if, in response to a 10% increase in income, the demand of a good increased by 20%, the _____ would be 20%/10% = 2.
    a. Indifference map
    b. Expenditure minimization problem
    c. Elasticity of substitution
    d. Income elasticity of demand

36. In economics, the _____ is defined as a numerical measure of the responsiveness of the quantity supplied of product (A) to a change in price of product (A) alone. It is the measure of the way quantity supplied reacts to a change in price.

    For example, if, in response to a 10% rise in the price of a good, the quantity supplied increases by 20%, the _____ would be 20%/10% = 2.

    a. Passive income
    b. Hedonimetry
    c. Price elasticity of supply
    d. Demand shaping

37. The supply of labor is the number of total hours that workers wish to work at a given real wage rate.

    _____ curves are derived from the 'labor-leisure' trade-off. More hours worked earn higher incomes but necessitate a cut in the amount of leisure that workers enjoy.

    a. Human trafficking
    b. Late capitalism
    c. Creative capitalism
    d. Labor supply

Chapter 5. Household Behavior and Consumer Choice

1. In economics, the term _____ of income or _____ refers to a simple economic model which describes the reciprocal circulation of income between producers and consumers. In the _____ model, the inter-dependent entities of producer and consumer are referred to as 'firms' and 'households' respectively and provide each other with factors in order to facilitate the flow of income. Firms provide consumers with goods and services in exchange for consumer expenditure and 'factors of production' from households.
   a. Circular flow
   b. 130-30 fund
   c. 1921 recession
   d. 100-year flood

2. _____ is the term denoting either an entrance or changes which are inserted into a system and which activate/modify a process. It is an abstract concept, used in the modeling, system(s) design and system(s) exploitation. It is usually connected with other terms, e.g., _____ field, _____ variable, _____ parameter, _____ value, _____ signal, _____ device and _____ file.
   a. ACCRA Cost of Living Index
   b. ACEA agreement
   c. AD-IA Model
   d. Input

3. _____s is the social science that studies the production, distribution, and consumption of goods and services. The term _____s comes from the Ancient Greek οἰκονομῐ́α from οἶκος (oikos, 'house') + νόμος (nomos, 'custom' or 'law'), hence 'rules of the house(hold)'. Current _____ models developed out of the broader field of political economy in the late 19th century, owing to a desire to use an empirical approach more akin to the physical sciences.
   a. Inflation
   b. Opportunity cost
   c. Economic
   d. Energy economics

4. In neoclassical economics and microeconomics, _____ describes the perfect being a market in which there are many small firms, all producing homogeneous goods. In the short term, such markets are productively inefficient as output will not occur where mc is equal to ac, but allocatively efficient, as output under _____ will always occur where mc is equal to mr, and therefore where mc equals ar. However, in the long term, such markets are both allocatively and productively efficient.
   a. Co-operative economics
   b. Law of supply
   c. General equilibrium
   d. Perfect competition

5. In economics, a _____ exists when a specific individual or enterprise has sufficient control over a particular product or service to determine significantly the terms on which other individuals shall have access to it. Monopolies are thus characterized by a lack of economic competition for the good or service that they provide and a lack of viable substitute goods. The verb 'monopolize' refers to the process by which a firm gains persistently greater market share than what is expected under perfect competition.
   a. 1921 recession
   b. 130-30 fund
   c. Monopoly
   d. 100-year flood

6. A _____ represents the combinations of goods and services that a consumer can purchase given current prices and his income. Consumer theory uses the concepts of a _____ and a preference map to analyze consumer choices. Both concepts have a ready graphical representation in the two-good case.
   a. Joint demand
   b. Revealed preference
   c. Quality bias
   d. Budget constraint

7. Cēterīs paribus is a Latin phrase, literally translated as 'with other things the same.' It is commonly rendered in English as 'all other things being equal.' A prediction, or a statement about causal or logical connections between two states of affairs, is qualified by _____ in order to acknowledge, and to rule out, the possibility of other factors which could override the relationship between the antecedent and the consequent.

Chapter 5. Household Behavior and Consumer Choice   35

A _____ assumption is often fundamental to the predictive purpose of scientific inquiry. In order to formulate scientific laws, it is usually necessary to rule out factors which interfere with examining a specific causal relationship.

a. Dematerialization
b. Friedman-Savage utility function
c. Ceteris paribus
d. Capital outflow

8. The _____ is 'the basic residential unit in which economic production, consumption, inheritance, child rearing, and shelter are organized and carried out'; [the _____] 'may or may not be synonymous with family'.

The _____ is the basic unit of analysis in many social, microeconomic and government models. The term refers to all individuals who live in the same dwelling.

a. 100-year flood
b. 130-30 fund
c. Family economics
d. Household

9. _____ is an economic model based on price, utility and quantity in a market. It predicts that in a competitive market, price will function to equalize the quantity demanded by consumers, and the quantity supplied by producers, resulting in an economic equilibrium of price and quantity. The model incorporates other factors changing equilibrium as a shift of demand and/or supply.

a. Joint demand
b. Rational addiction
c. Deferred gratification
d. Supply and demand

10. Economics:

- _____, the desire to own something and the ability to pay for it
- _____ curve, a graphic representation of a _____ schedule
- _____ deposit, the money in checking accounts
- _____ pull theory, the theory that inflation occurs when _____ for goods and services exceeds existing supplies
- _____ schedule, a table that lists the quantity of a good a person will buy it each different price
- _____ side economics, the school of economics at believes government spending and tax cuts open economy by raising _____

a. McKesson ' Robbins scandal
b. Production
c. Demand
d. Variability

11. In algebra, a _____ is a function depending on n that associates a scalar, det(A), to an n×n square matrix A. The fundamental geometric meaning of a _____ is a scale factor for measure when A is regarded as a linear transformation. _____s are important both in calculus, where they enter the substitution rule for several variables, and in multilinear algebra.

For a fixed nonnegative integer n, there is a unique _____ function for the n×n matrices over any commutative ring R. In particular, this function exists when R is the field of real or complex numbers.

a. 1921 recession
c. 130-30 fund
b. 100-year flood
d. Determinant

12. _____ in economics and business is the result of an exchange and from that trade we assign a numerical monetary value to a good, service or asset. If Alice trades Bob 4 apples for an orange, the _____ of an orange is 4 apples. Inversely, the _____ of an apple is 1/4 oranges.
   a. Price war
   c. Price book
   b. Premium pricing
   d. Price

13. A _____ is one scenario provided for evaluation by respondents in a Choice Experiment. Responses are collected and used to create a Choice Model. Respondents are usually provided with a series of differing _____s for evaluation.
   a. 100-year flood
   c. 130-30 fund
   b. Choice set
   d. 1921 recession

14. _____ or economic opportunity loss is the value of the next best alternative foregone as the result of making a decision. _____ analysis is an important part of a company's decision-making processes but is not treated as an actual cost in any financial statement. The next best thing that a person can engage in is referred to as the _____ of doing the best thing and ignoring the next best thing to be done.
   a. Economic ideology
   c. Economic
   b. Opportunity cost
   d. Industrial organization

15. A _____ is a situation that involves losing one quality or aspect of something in return for gaining another quality or aspect. It implies a decision to be made with full comprehension of both the upside and downside of a particular choice.

In economics the term is expressed as opportunity cost, referring the most preferred alternative given up.

   a. Whitemail
   c. Nonmarket
   b. Trade-off
   d. Friedman-Savage utility function

16. In management accounting, _____ establishes budget and actual cost of operations, processes, departments or product and the analysis of variances, profitability or social use of funds. Managers use _____ to support decision-making to cut a company's costs and improve profitability. As a form of management accounting, _____ need not follow standards such as GAAP, because its primary use is for internal managers, rather than outside users, and what to compute is instead decided pragmatically.
   a. Quality costs
   c. Cost accounting
   b. Total absorption costing
   d. Khozraschyot

17. In economics, _____ is a measure of the relative satisfaction from consumption of various goods and services. Given this measure, one may speak meaningfully of increasing or decreasing _____, and thereby explain economic behavior in terms of attempts to increase one's _____. For illustrative purposes, changes in _____ are sometimes expressed in units called utils.
   a. Utility
   c. Expected utility hypothesis
   b. Utility function
   d. Ordinal utility

18. In economics, the _____ of a good or of a service is the utility of the specific use to which an agent would put a given increase in that good or service, or of the specific use that would be abandoned in response to a given decrease. In other words, _____ is the utility of the marginal use -- which, on the assumption of economic rationality, would be the least urgent use of the good or service, from the best feasible combination of actions in which its use is included. Under the mainstream assumptions, the _____ of a good or service is the posited quantified change in utility obtained by increasing or by decreasing use of that good or service.
    a. 130-30 fund
    b. Marginal utility
    c. 100-year flood
    d. 1921 recession

Chapter 5. Household Behavior and Consumer Choice

19. A _____ is:

- Rewrite _____, in generative grammar and computer science
- Standardization, a formal and widely-accepted statement, fact, definition, or qualification
- Operation, a determinate _____ for performing a mathematical operation and obtaining a certain result (Mathematics, Logic)
    - Unary operation
    - Binary operation
- _____ of inference, a function from sets of formulae to formulae (Mathematics, Logic)
- _____ of thumb, principle with broad application that is not intended to be strictly accurate or reliable for every situation. Also often simply referred to as a _____
- Moral, an atomic element of a moral code for guiding choices in human behavior
- Heuristic, a quantized '_____' which shows a tendency or probability for successful function
- A regulation, as in sports
- A Production _____, as in computer science
- Procedural law, a _____ set governing the application of laws to cases
    - A law, which may informally be called a '_____'
    - A court ruling, a decision by a court
- In the U.S. Government, a regulation mandated by Congress, but written or expanded upon by the Executive Branch.
- Norm (sociology), an informal but widely accepted _____, concept, truth, definition, or qualification (social norms, legal norms, coding norms)
- Norm (philosophy), a kind of sentence or a reason to act, feel or believe
- 'Rulership' is the concept of governance by a government:
    - Military _____, governance by a military body
    - Monastic _____, a collection of precepts that guides the life of monks or nuns in a religious order where the superior holds the place of Christ
- Slide _____

- '_____,' a song by Ayumi Hamasaki
- '_____,' a song by rapper Nas
- '_____s,' an album by the band The Whitest Boy Alive
- _____s: Pyaar Ka Superhit Formula, a 2003 Bollywood film
- ruler, an instrument for measuring lengths
- _____, a component of an astrolabe, circumferator or similar instrument
- The _____s, a bestselling self-help book
- _____ Project (Run Up-to-date Linux Everywhere), a project that aims to use up-to-date Linux software on old PCs
- _____ engine, a software system that helps managing business _____s
- Ja _____, a hip hop artist
    - R.U.L.E., a 2005 greatest hits album by rapper Ja _____
- '_____s,' a KMFDM song

a. Procter ' Gamble
b. Technocracy
c. Demand
d. Rule

Chapter 5. Household Behavior and Consumer Choice

20. In economics, the _____ can be defined as the graph depicting the relationship between the price of a certain commodity, and the amount of it that consumers are willing and able to purchase at that given price. It is a graphic representation of a demand schedule. The _____ for all consumers together follows from the _____ of every individual consumer: the individual demands at each price are added together.
   a. Wage curve
   b. Demand curve
   c. Cost curve
   d. Kuznets curve

21. A _____ is an object whose consumption increases the utility of the consumer, for which the quantity demanded exceeds the quantity supplied at zero price. _____s are usually modeled as having diminishing marginal utility. The first individual purchase has high utility; the second has less.
   a. Merit good
   b. Good
   c. Pie method
   d. Composite good

22. In economics, the _____ is the change in consumption resulting from a change in real income.

Another important item that can change is the money income of the consumer. The _____ is the phenomenon observed through changes in purchasing power.

   a. Income effect
   b. Export subsidy
   c. Equilibrium wage
   d. Inflation hedge

23. In economics, _____s are any goods for which demand increases when income increases and falls when income decreases but price remains constant, i.e. with a positive income elasticity of demand. The term does not necessarily refer to the quality of the good.

Depending on the indifference curves, the amount of a good bought can either increase, decrease, or stay the same when income increases.

   a. Bord halfpenny
   b. Financial contagion
   c. Normative economics
   d. Normal good

24. A _____ is a theoretical term that economists use to describe a market which is free from government intervention (i.e. no regulation, no subsidization, no single monetary system and no governmental monopolies.) In a _____, property rights are voluntarily exchanged at a price arranged solely by the mutual consent of sellers and buyers. By definition, buyers and sellers do not coerce each other, in the sense that they obtain each other's property without the use of physical force, threat of physical force, or fraud, nor is the coerced by a third party (such as by government via transfer payments) and they engage in trade simply because they both consent and believe that it is a good enough choice.
   a. Leninism
   b. Delegation
   c. Third camp
   d. Free market

25. _____ is a broad label that refers to any individuals or households that use goods and services generated within the economy. The concept of a _____ is used in different contexts, so that the usage and significance of the term may vary.

Typically when business people and economists talk of _____s they are talking about person as _____, an aggregated commodity item with little individuality other than that expressed in the buy/not-buy decision.

a. 1921 recession
c. 130-30 fund
b. 100-year flood
d. Consumer

26. The term surplus is used in economics for several related quantities. The _____ is the amount that consumers benefit by being able to purchase a product for a price that is less than they would be willing to pay. The producer surplus is the amount that producers benefit by selling at a market price mechanism that is higher than they would be willing to sell for.

a. Marginal rate of technical substitution
c. Necessity good
b. Microeconomic reform
d. Consumer surplus

27. _____ was a survey conducted by the U.S. Department of Justice to gauge the prevalence of alcohol and illegal drug use among prior arrestees. It was a reformulation of the prior Drug Use Forecasting (DUF) program, focused on five drugs in particular: cocaine, marijuana, methamphetamine, opiates, and PCP.

Participants were randomly selected from arrest records in major metropolitan areas; because no personally identifying information is taken from each record chosen, the resulting data can be correlated to arrest rates, but not to the total population of persons charged.

a. Arrestee Drug Abuse Monitoring
c. ACCRA Cost of Living Index
b. AD-IA Model
d. ACEA agreement

28. _____ is a term that refers both to:

- a formal discipline used to help appraise, or assess, the case for a project or proposal, which itself is a process known as project appraisal; and
- an informal approach to making decisions of any kind.

Under both definitions the process involves, whether explicitly or implicitly, weighing the total expected costs against the total expected benefits of one or more actions in order to choose the best or most profitable option. The formal process is often referred to as either CBA (_____) or BCost-benefit analysis

A hallmark of CBA is that all benefits and all costs are expressed in money terms, and are adjusted for the time value of money, so that all flows of benefits and flows of project costs over time (which tend to occur at different points in time) are expressed on a common basis in terms of their e;present value.e; Closely related, but slightly different, formal techniques include Cost-effectiveness analysis, Economic impact analysis, Fiscal impact analysis and Social Return on Investment(SROI) analysis. The latter builds upon the logic of _____, but differs in that it is explicitly designed to inform the practical decision-making of enterprise managers and investors focused on optimising their social and environmental impacts.

a. 100-year flood
b. Cost-benefit analysis
c. Decision theory
d. 130-30 fund

29. _____ was a Scottish moral philosopher and a pioneer of political economy. One of the key figures of the Scottish Enlightenment, Smith is the author of The Theory of Moral Sentiments and An Inquiry into the Nature and Causes of the Wealth of Nations. The latter, usually abbreviated as The Wealth of Nations, is considered his magnum opus and the first modern work of economics.
   a. Adolf Hitler
   b. Alan Greenspan
   c. Adolph Fischer
   d. Adam Smith

30. The _____ is the apparent contradiction that although water is on the whole more useful, in terms of survival, than diamonds, diamonds command a higher price in the market. The economist Adam Smith is often considered to be the classic presenter of this paradox. Nicolaus Copernicus, John Locke, John Law and others had previously tried to explain the disparity.
   a. 130-30 fund
   b. 100-year flood
   c. Paradox of value
   d. St. Petersburg paradox

31. The supply of labor is the number of total hours that workers wish to work at a given real wage rate.

   _____ curves are derived from the 'labor-leisure' trade-off. More hours worked earn higher incomes but necessitate a cut in the amount of leisure that workers enjoy.

   a. Human trafficking
   b. Late capitalism
   c. Creative capitalism
   d. Labor supply

32. _____ is a common concept in economics, and gives rise to derived concepts such as consumer debt. Generally _____ is defined by opposition to production. But the precise definition can vary because different schools of economists define production quite differently.
   a. Cash or share options
   b. Foreclosure data providers
   c. Federal Reserve Bank Notes
   d. Consumption

33. The _____ is the market for securities, where companies and governments can raise longterm funds. It is a market in which money is lent for periods longer than a year. The _____ includes the stock market and the bond market.
   a. Financial instrument
   b. Performance attribution
   c. Multi-family office
   d. Capital market

34. In microeconomic theory, an _____ is a graph showing different bundles of goods, each measured as to quantity, between which a consumer is indifferent. That is, at each point on the curve, the consumer has no preference for one bundle over another. In other words, they are all equally preferred.
   a. Engel curve
   b. Indifference curve
   c. Indifference map
   d. Expenditure minimization problem

35. In economics, the _____ is the rate at which a consumer is ready to give up one good in exchange for another good while maintaining the same level of satisfaction.

Under the standard assumption of neoclassical economics that goods and services are continuously divisible, the marginal rates of substitution will be the same regardless of the direction of exchange, and will correspond to the slope of an indifference curve (more precisely, to the slope multiplied by -1) passing through the consumption bundle in question, at that point: mathematically, it is the implicit derivative. MRS of Y for X is the amount of Y for which a consumer is willing to exchange for X locally.

   a. Marginal rate of substitution
   b. Demand vacuum
   c. Supply and demand
   d. Quality bias

36. In microeconomic theory a _____ or indifference map is the collection of indifference curves possessed by an individual. Similar in nature to a topographical map, the contour lines of such a map demonstrating progressively more desirable options as they move upward or to the right. Because of the nature of indifference curves they cannot intersect and are effectively infinite in number, their sum defining all possible combinations of values.
   a. Preference map
   b. Marginal rate of substitution
   c. Deferred gratification
   d. Cross elasticity of demand

Chapter 6. The Production Process: The Behavior of Profit-Maximizing Firms

1. In microeconomics, _____ is quite simply the conversion of inputs into outputs. It is an economic process that uses resources to create a good or service that is suitable for exchange. This can include manufacturing, storing, shipping, and packaging.
   a. MET
   b. Red Guards
   c. Solved
   d. Production

2. In neoclassical economics and microeconomics, _____ describes the perfect being a market in which there are many small firms, all producing homogeneous goods. In the short term, such markets are productively inefficient as output will not occur where mc is equal to ac, but allocatively efficient, as output under _____ will always occur where mc is equal to mr, and therefore where mc equals ar. However, in the long term, such markets are both allocatively and productively efficient.
   a. General equilibrium
   b. Co-operative economics
   c. Law of supply
   d. Perfect competition

3. In economics, a _____ exists when a specific individual or enterprise has sufficient control over a particular product or service to determine significantly the terms on which other individuals shall have access to it. Monopolies are thus characterized by a lack of economic competition for the good or service that they provide and a lack of viable substitute goods. The verb 'monopolize' refers to the process by which a firm gains persistently greater market share than what is expected under perfect competition.
   a. 130-30 fund
   b. 100-year flood
   c. Monopoly
   d. 1921 recession

4. _____s is the social science that studies the production, distribution, and consumption of goods and services. The term _____s comes from the Ancient Greek οἰκονομῖα from οἶκος (oikos, 'house') + νόμος (nomos, 'custom' or 'law'), hence 'rules of the house(hold)'. Current _____ models developed out of the broader field of political economy in the late 19th century, owing to a desire to use an empirical approach more akin to the physical sciences.
   a. Opportunity cost
   b. Energy economics
   c. Inflation
   d. Economic

5. The _____ of a decision depends on both the cost of the alternative chosen and the benefit that the best alternative would have provided if chosen. _____ differs from accounting cost because it includes opportunity cost.
   a. Epstein-Zin preferences
   b. Isocost
   c. Inventory analysis
   d. Economic cost

6. An _____ is an easy accounted cost, such as wage, rent and materials. It can be transacted in the form of money payment and is lost directly, as opposed to monetary implicit costs.
   a. Explicit cost
   b. Average variable cost
   c. Average fixed cost
   d. Inventory valuation

7. In economics, an _____ occurs when one foregoes an alternative action but does not make an actual payment. (For instance, the explicit cost of a night at the movies includes the moviegoer's ticket and soda, but the _____ includes the pay he would have earned if he had chosen to work instead.) _____s are related to forgone benefits of any single transaction.
   a. External sector
   b. Ostrich strategy
   c. Implicit cost
   d. Overnight trade

Chapter 6. The Production Process: The Behavior of Profit-Maximizing Firms

8. _____ or economic opportunity loss is the value of the next best alternative foregone as the result of making a decision. _____ analysis is an important part of a company's decision-making processes but is not treated as an actual cost in any financial statement. The next best thing that a person can engage in is referred to as the _____ of doing the best thing and ignoring the next best thing to be done.
   a. Opportunity cost
   b. Economic ideology
   c. Industrial organization
   d. Economic

9. _____ are direct outlays of cash which may or may not be later reimbursed.

In operating a vehicle, gasoline, parking fees and tolls are considered _____ for the trip. Insurance, oil changes, and interest are not, because the outlay of cash covers expenses accrued over a longer period of time.

   a. Out-of-pocket expenses
   b. AD-IA Model
   c. ACCRA Cost of Living Index
   d. ACEA agreement

10. In economics, and cost accounting, _____ describes the total economic cost of production and is made up of variable costs, which vary according to the quantity of a good produced and include inputs such as labor and raw materials, plus fixed costs, which are independent of the quantity of a good produced and include inputs (capital) that cannot be varied in the short term, such as buildings and machinery. _____ in economics includes the total opportunity cost of each factor of production in addition to fixed and variable costs.

The rate at which _____ changes as the amount produced changes is called marginal cost.

   a. 130-30 fund
   b. 100-year flood
   c. 1921 recession
   d. Total cost

11. _____ is the total money received from the sale of any given quantity of output.

The _____ is calculated by taking the price of the sale times the quantity sold, i.e.

_____ = price X quantity.

   a. Small numbers game
   b. Market development funds
   c. Ceteris paribus
   d. Total revenue

12. In management accounting, _____ establishes budget and actual cost of operations, processes, departments or product and the analysis of variances, profitability or social use of funds. Managers use _____ to support decision-making to cut a company's costs and improve profitability. As a form of management accounting, _____ need not follow standards such as GAAP, because its primary use is for internal managers, rather than outside users, and what to compute is instead decided pragmatically.
   a. Khozraschyot
   b. Total absorption costing
   c. Quality costs
   d. Cost accounting

Chapter 6. The Production Process: The Behavior of Profit-Maximizing Firms

13. In finance, _____ rate of profit or sometimes just return, is the ratio of money gained or lost on an investment relative to the amount of money invested. The amount of money gained or lost may be referred to as interest, profit/loss, gain/loss, or net income/loss. The money invested may be referred to as the asset, capital, principal, or the cost basis of the investment.
    a. Cost accrual ratio
    b. Sortino ratio
    c. Rate of return
    d. Current ratio

14. In economic models, the _____ time frame assumes no fixed factors of production. Firms can enter or leave the marketplace, and the cost (and availability) of land, labor, raw materials, and capital goods can be assumed to vary. In contrast, in the short-run time frame, certain factors are assumed to be fixed, because there is not sufficient time for them to change.
    a. Price/performance ratio
    b. Productivity world
    c. Diseconomies of scale
    d. Long-run

15. In economics, the concept of the _____ refers to the decision-making time frame of a firm in which at least one factor of production is fixed. Costs which are fixed in the _____ have no impact on a firms decisions. For example a firm can raise output by increasing the amount of labour through overtime.
    a. Hicks-neutral technical change
    b. Product Pipeline
    c. Productivity model
    d. Short-run

16. In economics, a _____ is a function that specifies the output of a firm, an industry, or an entire economy for all combinations of inputs. A meta-_____ compares the practice of the existing entities converting inputs X into output y to determine the most efficient practice _____ of the existing entities, whether the most efficient feasible practice production or the most efficient actual practice production. In either case, the maximum output of a technologically-determined production process is a mathematical function of input factors of production.
    a. Production function
    b. Constant elasticity of substitution
    c. Post-Fordism
    d. Short-run

17. The _____ of a variable factor of Production identifies what outputs are possible using various levels of the variable input. This can be displayed in either a chart that lists the output level corresponding to various levels of input, or a graph that summarizes the data into a '_____ curve'. The diagram shows a typical _____ curve. In this example, output increases as more inputs are employed up until point A. The maximum output possible with this Production process is Qm. (If there are other inputs used in the process, they are assumed to be fixed).
    a. Total product
    b. Tightness
    c. Convexity
    d. Consequence

18. In economics, the _____ or marginal physical product is the extra output produced by one more unit of an input (for instance, the difference in output when a firm's labour is increased from five to six units.) Assuming that no other inputs to production change, the _____ of a given input (X) can be expressed as:

    _____ = $\Delta Y / \Delta X$ = (the change of Y)/(the change of X.)

-
  -
    - Pending approval by Thomas Sowell***

Chapter 6. The Production Process: The Behavior of Profit-Maximizing Firms

In neoclassical economics, this is the mathematical derivative of the production function.... Note that the 'product' (Y) is typically defined ignoring external costs and benefits.

a. Labor problem
b. Factor prices
c. Productive capacity
d. Marginal product

19. In economics, _____ refers to how the marginal contribution of a factor of production usually decreases as more of the factor is used. According to this relationship, in a production system with fixed and variable inputs, beyond some point, each additional unit of the variable input yields smaller and smaller increases in output. Conversely, producing one more unit of output costs more and more in variable inputs.

a. Patent troll
b. Community property
c. Derivatives law
d. Diminishing returns

20. In economics, _____ are the resources employed to produce goods and services. They facilitate production but do not become part of the product (as with raw materials) or significantly transformed by the production process (as with fuel used to power machinery.) To 19th century economists, the _____ were land (natural resources, gifts from nature), labor (the ability to work), and capital goods (human-made tools and equipment.)

a. Hicks-neutral technical change
b. Factors of production
c. Long-run
d. Product Pipeline

21. _____ is the term denoting either an entrance or changes which are inserted into a system and which activate/modify a process. It is an abstract concept, used in the modeling, system(s) design and system(s) exploitation. It is usually connected with other terms, e.g., _____ field, _____ variable, _____ parameter, _____ value, _____ signal, _____ device and _____ file.

a. AD-IA Model
b. ACCRA Cost of Living Index
c. ACEA agreement
d. Input

22. In calculus, a function f defined on a subset of the real numbers with real values is called _____, if for all x and y such that x >≤ y one has f(x) >≤ f(y), so f preserves the order. In layman's terms, the sign of the slope is always positive (the curve tending upwards) or zero (i.e., non-decreasing, or asymptotic, or depicted as a horizontal, flat line) Likewise, a function is called monotonically decreasing (non-increasing) if, whenever x >≤ y, then f(x) >≥ f(y), so it reverses the order.

a. 100-year flood
b. 1921 recession
c. 130-30 fund
d. Monotonic

23. _____ in economics refers to metrics and measures of output from production processes, per unit of input. Labor _____, for example, is typically measured as a ratio of output per labor-hour, an input. _____ may be conceived of as a metrics of the technical or engineering efficiency of production.

a. Production-possibility frontier
b. Fordism
c. Piece work
d. Productivity

24. In economics, an _____ is a contour line drawn through the set of points at which the same quantity of output is produced while changing the quantities of two or more inputs. While an indifference curve helps to answer the utility-maximizing problem of consumers, the _____ deals with the cost-minimization problem of producers. _____s are typically drawn on capital-labor graphs, showing the tradeoff between capital and labor in the production function, and the decreasing marginal returns of both inputs.

Chapter 6. The Production Process: The Behavior of Profit-Maximizing Firms

a. Economic production quantity
b. Isoquant
c. Underinvestment employment relationship
d. Economies of scale

25. _____ is the additional output resulting from the use of an additional unit of capital (ceteris paribus assuming all other factors are fixed.) It equals to 1 divided by the Incremental Capital-Output Ratio.
   a. Buy-write
   b. CAN SLIM
   c. Loan officer
   d. Marginal product of capital

26. In economics an _____ line represents a combination of inputs which all cost the same amount. Although similar to the budget constraint in consumer theory, the use of the _____ pertains to cost-minimization in production, as opposed to utility-maximization. The typical _____ line represents the ratio of costs of labour and capital, so the formula is often written as:

$$rK + wL = C$$

Where w represents the wage of labour, and r represents the rental rate of capital.

   a. Epstein-Zin preferences
   b. Inventory analysis
   c. Isocost
   d. Incentive

27. In economics, the _____ is the rate at which a consumer is ready to give up one good in exchange for another good while maintaining the same level of satisfaction.

Under the standard assumption of neoclassical economics that goods and services are continuously divisible, the marginal rates of substitution will be the same regardless of the direction of exchange, and will correspond to the slope of an indifference curve (more precisely, to the slope multiplied by -1) passing through the consumption bundle in question, at that point: mathematically, it is the implicit derivative. MRS of Y for X is the amount of Y for which a consumer is willing to exchange for X locally.

   a. Marginal rate of substitution
   b. Supply and demand
   c. Quality bias
   d. Demand vacuum

Chapter 7. Short-Run Costs and Output Decisions

1. In economics, the term _____ of income or _____ refers to a simple economic model which describes the reciprocal circulation of income between producers and consumers. In the _____ model, the inter-dependent entities of producer and consumer are referred to as 'firms' and 'households' respectively and provide each other with factors in order to facilitate the flow of income. Firms provide consumers with goods and services in exchange for consumer expenditure and 'factors of production' from households.
   a. Circular flow
   b. 100-year flood
   c. 1921 recession
   d. 130-30 fund

2. _____ is the term denoting either an entrance or changes which are inserted into a system and which activate/modify a process. It is an abstract concept, used in the modeling, system(s) design and system(s) exploitation. It is usually connected with other terms, e.g., _____ field, _____ variable, _____ parameter, _____ value, _____ signal, _____ device and _____ file.
   a. ACCRA Cost of Living Index
   b. ACEA agreement
   c. AD-IA Model
   d. Input

3. _____ or economic opportunity loss is the value of the next best alternative foregone as the result of making a decision. _____ analysis is an important part of a company's decision-making processes but is not treated as an actual cost in any financial statement. The next best thing that a person can engage in is referred to as the _____ of doing the best thing and ignoring the next best thing to be done.
   a. Economic ideology
   b. Economic
   c. Opportunity cost
   d. Industrial organization

4. In management accounting, _____ establishes budget and actual cost of operations, processes, departments or product and the analysis of variances, profitability or social use of funds. Managers use _____ to support decision-making to cut a company's costs and improve profitability. As a form of management accounting, _____ need not follow standards such as GAAP, because its primary use is for internal managers, rather than outside users, and what to compute is instead decided pragmatically.
   a. Khozraschyot
   b. Cost accounting
   c. Quality costs
   d. Total absorption costing

5. _____s is the social science that studies the production, distribution, and consumption of goods and services. The term _____s comes from the Ancient Greek οἰκονομία from οἶκος (oikos, 'house') + νόμος (nomos, 'custom' or 'law'), hence 'rules of the house(hold)'. Current _____ models developed out of the broader field of political economy in the late 19th century, owing to a desire to use an empirical approach more akin to the physical sciences.
   a. Inflation
   b. Energy economics
   c. Opportunity cost
   d. Economic

6. In economics, _____ are business expenses that are not dependent on the activities of the business They tend to be time-related, such as salaries or rents being paid per month. This is in contrast to variable costs, which are volume-related (and are paid per quantity.)

In management accounting, _____ are defined as expenses that do not change in proportion to the activity of a business, within the relevant period or scale of production.

   a. Quality costs
   b. Cost of poor quality
   c. Fixed costs
   d. Cost-Volume-Profit Analysis

Chapter 7. Short-Run Costs and Output Decisions

7. In economics, and cost accounting, _____ describes the total economic cost of production and is made up of variable costs, which vary according to the quantity of a good produced and include inputs such as labor and raw materials, plus fixed costs, which are independent of the quantity of a good produced and include inputs (capital) that cannot be varied in the short term, such as buildings and machinery. _____ in economics includes the total opportunity cost of each factor of production in addition to fixed and variable costs.

The rate at which _____ changes as the amount produced changes is called marginal cost.

   a. 130-30 fund
   b. 100-year flood
   c. Total cost
   d. 1921 recession

8. _____s are expenses that change in proportion to the activity of a business. In other words, _____ is the sum of marginal costs. It can also be considered normal costs.
   a. Cost allocation
   b. Cost-Volume-Profit Analysis
   c. Variable cost
   d. Quality costs

9. _____ is an economics term used to describe the total fixed costs (TFC) divided by the quantity (Q) of units produced.

$$AFC = \frac{TFC}{Q}$$

_____ is a per-unit measure of fixed costs. As the total number of goods produced increases, the _____ decreases because the same amount of fixed costs are being spread over a larger number of units.

   a. Inventory valuation
   b. Average variable cost
   c. Explicit cost
   d. Average fixed cost

10. In business, _____, Overhead cost or _____ expense refers to an ongoing expense of operating a business. The term _____ is usually used to group expenses that are necessary to the continued functioning of the business, but do not directly generate profits.

_____ expenses are all costs on the income statement except for direct labor and direct materials.

   a. ACEA agreement
   b. AD-IA Model
   c. ACCRA Cost of Living Index
   d. Overhead

11. In economics and business decision-making, _____ are costs that cannot be recovered once they have been incurred. _____ are sometimes contrasted with variable costs, which are the costs that will change due to the proposed course of action, and prospective costs which are costs that will be incurred if an action is taken.

In traditional microeconomic theory, only variable costs are relevant to a decision.

a. Halo effect
b. Post-purchase rationalization
c. Hyperbolic discounting
d. Sunk costs

12. In economics, a _____ is a graph of the costs of production as a function of total quantity produced. In a free market economy, productively efficient firms use these curves to find the optimal point of production, where they make the most profits. There are a few different types of _____s, each relevant to a different area of economics.

a. Demand curve
b. Cost curve
c. Phillips curve
d. Kuznets curve

13. In economics and finance, _____ is the change in total cost that arises when the quantity produced changes by one unit. It is the cost of producing one more unit of a good. Mathematically, the _____ function is expressed as the first derivative of the total cost (TC) function with respect to quantity (Q.)

a. Quality costs
b. Variable cost
c. Khozraschyot
d. Marginal cost

14. To _____ is to impose a financial charge or other levy upon a taxpayer by a state or the functional equivalent of a state.

_____es are also imposed by many subnational entities. _____es consist of direct _____ or indirect _____, and may be paid in money or as its labour equivalent (often but not always unpaid.)

a. Tax
b. 130-30 fund
c. 1921 recession
d. 100-year flood

15. _____ is an economics term to describe a firms variable costs (labor, electricity, etc.) divided by the quantity (Q) of total units of output.

$$AVC = \frac{TVC}{Q}$$

Where:

- TVC = Total Variable Cost
- _____ = Average variable cost
- Q = Quantity of Units Produced

_____ plus average fixed cost equals average total cost:

_____ + AFC = ATC.

a. Inventory valuation
b. Explicit cost
c. Average variable cost
d. Average fixed cost

Chapter 7. Short-Run Costs and Output Decisions

16. In economics, _____ is the process by which a firm determines the price and output level that returns the greatest profit. There are several approaches to this problem. The total revenue--total cost method relies on the fact that profit equals revenue minus cost, and the marginal revenue--marginal cost method is based on the fact that total profit in a perfectly competitive market reaches its maximum point where marginal revenue equals marginal cost.
    a. Profit margin
    b. Profit maximization
    c. Normal profit
    d. 100-year flood

17. Economics:

    - _____, the desire to own something and the ability to pay for it
    - _____ curve, a graphic representation of a _____ schedule
    - _____ deposit, the money in checking accounts
    - _____ pull theory, the theory that inflation occurs when _____ for goods and services exceeds existing supplies
    - _____ schedule, a table that lists the quantity of a good a person will buy it each different price
    - _____ side economics, the school of economics at believes government spending and tax cuts open economy by raising _____

    a. Production
    b. McKesson ' Robbins scandal
    c. Variability
    d. Demand

18. In economics, the _____ can be defined as the graph depicting the relationship between the price of a certain commodity, and the amount of it that consumers are willing and able to purchase at that given price. It is a graphic representation of a demand schedule. The _____ for all consumers together follows from the _____ of every individual consumer: the individual demands at each price are added together.
    a. Wage curve
    b. Kuznets curve
    c. Cost curve
    d. Demand curve

19. In microeconomics, _____ is the extra revenue that an additional unit of product will bring. It is the additional income from selling one more unit of a good; sometimes equal to price. It can also be described as the change in total revenue/change in number of units sold.
    a. Marginal revenue
    b. Long term
    c. Reservation price
    d. Market demand schedule

20. _____ is the total money received from the sale of any given quantity of output.

The _____ is calculated by taking the price of the sale times the quantity sold, i.e.

_____ = price X quantity.

    a. Small numbers game
    b. Ceteris paribus
    c. Market development funds
    d. Total revenue

21. In economics, the concept of the _____ refers to the decision-making time frame of a firm in which at least one factor of production is fixed. Costs which are fixed in the _____ have no impact on a firms decisions. For example a firm can raise output by increasing the amount of labour through overtime.
    a. Productivity model   b. Short-run
    c. Product Pipeline   d. Hicks-neutral technical change

Chapter 8. Long-Run Costs and Output Decisions

1. In economics and business, specifically cost accounting, the _____ point (BEP) is the point at which cost or expenses and revenue are equal: there is no net loss or gain, and one has 'broken even'. A profit or a loss has not been made, although opportunity costs have been paid, and capital has received the risk-adjusted, expected return.

   For example, if the business sells less than 200 tables each month, it will make a loss, if it sells more, it will be a profit.

   a. Nonmarket
   b. Small numbers game
   c. Break-even
   d. Buffer stock scheme

2. In economic models, the _____ time frame assumes no fixed factors of production. Firms can enter or leave the marketplace, and the cost (and availability) of land, labor, raw materials, and capital goods can be assumed to vary. In contrast, in the short-run time frame, certain factors are assumed to be fixed, because there is not sufficient time for them to change.
   a. Long-run
   b. Diseconomies of scale
   c. Price/performance ratio
   d. Productivity world

3. In economics, _____ is the process by which a firm determines the price and output level that returns the greatest profit. There are several approaches to this problem. The total revenue--total cost method relies on the fact that profit equals revenue minus cost, and the marginal revenue--marginal cost method is based on the fact that total profit in a perfectly competitive market reaches its maximum point where marginal revenue equals marginal cost.
   a. 100-year flood
   b. Normal profit
   c. Profit margin
   d. Profit maximization

4. In economics, the concept of the _____ refers to the decision-making time frame of a firm in which at least one factor of production is fixed. Costs which are fixed in the _____ have no impact on a firms decisions. For example a firm can raise output by increasing the amount of labour through overtime.
   a. Hicks-neutral technical change
   b. Short-run
   c. Product Pipeline
   d. Productivity model

5. In finance, _____ rate of profit or sometimes just return, is the ratio of money gained or lost on an investment relative to the amount of money invested. The amount of money gained or lost may be referred to as interest, profit/loss, gain/loss, or net income/loss. The money invested may be referred to as the asset, capital, principal, or the cost basis of the investment.
   a. Cost accrual ratio
   b. Current ratio
   c. Sortino ratio
   d. Rate of return

6. _____ is the total money received from the sale of any given quantity of output.

   The _____ is calculated by taking the price of the sale times the quantity sold, i.e.

   _____ = price X quantity.

   a. Ceteris paribus
   b. Total revenue
   c. Market development funds
   d. Small numbers game

Chapter 8. Long-Run Costs and Output Decisions

7. _____ is a term variously used for approaches to economics focusing on the determination of prices, outputs, and income distributions in markets through supply and demand, often as mediated through a hypothesized maximization of income-constrained utility by individuals and of cost-constrained profits of firms employing available information and factors of production, in accordance with rational choice theory. _____ dominates microeconomics, and together with Keynesian economics forms the neoclassical synthesis, which dominates mainstream economics today. There have been many critiques of _____, often incorporated into newer versions of neoclassical theory as human awareness of economic criteria change.

   a. Price theory
   b. Neoclassical economics
   c. Law of supply
   d. Keynesian theory

8. _____ is a measure of a company's earning power from ongoing operations, equal to earnings before the deduction of interest payments and income taxes.

To accountants, economic profit, or EP, is a single-period metric to determine the value created by a company in one period - usually a year. It is the net profit after tax less the equity charge, a risk-weighted cost of capital.

   a. Economic profit
   b. Accounting profit
   c. ACCRA Cost of Living Index
   d. Operating profit

9. _____ or economic opportunity loss is the value of the next best alternative foregone as the result of making a decision. _____ analysis is an important part of a company's decision-making processes but is not treated as an actual cost in any financial statement. The next best thing that a person can engage in is referred to as the _____ of doing the best thing and ignoring the next best thing to be done.

   a. Opportunity cost
   b. Economic
   c. Industrial organization
   d. Economic ideology

10. In economics, and cost accounting, _____ describes the total economic cost of production and is made up of variable costs, which vary according to the quantity of a good produced and include inputs such as labor and raw materials, plus fixed costs, which are independent of the quantity of a good produced and include inputs (capital) that cannot be varied in the short term, such as buildings and machinery. _____ in economics includes the total opportunity cost of each factor of production in addition to fixed and variable costs.

The rate at which _____ changes as the amount produced changes is called marginal cost.

   a. Total cost
   b. 1921 recession
   c. 100-year flood
   d. 130-30 fund

11. _____ is a broad label that refers to any individuals or households that use goods and services generated within the economy. The concept of a _____ is used in different contexts, so that the usage and significance of the term may vary.

Typically when business people and economists talk of _____s they are talking about person as _____, an aggregated commodity item with little individuality other than that expressed in the buy/not-buy decision.

Chapter 8. Long-Run Costs and Output Decisions

    a. 100-year flood
    c. 1921 recession
    b. 130-30 fund
    d. Consumer

12. In management accounting, _____ establishes budget and actual cost of operations, processes, departments or product and the analysis of variances, profitability or social use of funds. Managers use _____ to support decision-making to cut a company's costs and improve profitability. As a form of management accounting, _____ need not follow standards such as GAAP, because its primary use is for internal managers, rather than outside users, and what to compute is instead decided pragmatically.
    a. Total absorption costing
    c. Quality costs
    b. Khozraschyot
    d. Cost accounting

13. _____s is the social science that studies the production, distribution, and consumption of goods and services. The term _____s comes from the Ancient Greek oá¼°κονομῖα from oá¼¶κος (oikos, 'house') + vÏŒμος (nomos, 'custom' or 'law'), hence 'rules of the house(hold)'. Current _____ models developed out of the broader field of political economy in the late 19th century, owing to a desire to use an empirical approach more akin to the physical sciences.
    a. Energy economics
    c. Inflation
    b. Economic
    d. Opportunity cost

14. In economics, _____ are business expenses that are not dependent on the activities of the business They tend to be time-related, such as salaries or rents being paid per month. This is in contrast to variable costs, which are volume-related (and are paid per quantity.)

In management accounting, _____ are defined as expenses that do not change in proportion to the activity of a business, within the relevant period or scale of production.

    a. Quality costs
    c. Fixed costs
    b. Cost-Volume-Profit Analysis
    d. Cost of poor quality

15. In economics, _____ is equal to total cost divided by the number of goods produced (the output quantity, Q.) It is also equal to the sum of average variable costs (total variable costs divided by Q) plus average fixed costs (total fixed costs divided by Q.) _____s may be dependent on the time period considered (increasing production may be expensive or impossible in the short term, for example.)
    a. Average variable cost
    c. Explicit cost
    b. Average fixed cost
    d. Average cost

16. In economics, a _____ is a graph of the costs of production as a function of total quantity produced. In a free market economy, productively efficient firms use these curves to find the optimal point of production, where they make the most profits. There are a few different types of _____s, each relevant to a different area of economics.
    a. Cost curve
    c. Phillips curve
    b. Demand curve
    d. Kuznets curve

17. In production, returns to scale refers to changes in output subsequent to a proportional change in all inputs (where all inputs increase by a constant factor.) If output increases by that same proportional change then there are _____ If output increases by less than that proportional change, there are decreasing returns to scale (DRS.)

a. Lexicographic preferences
b. Consumer sovereignty
c. Long term
d. Constant returns to scale

18. _____ are the forces that cause larger firms to produce goods and services at increased per-unit costs. They are less well known than what economists have long understood as 'economies of scale', the forces which enable larger firms to produce goods and services at reduced per-unit costs.

Some of the forces which cause a diseconomy of scale are listed below:

Ideally, all employees of a firm would have one-on-one communication with each other so they know exactly what the other workers are doing.

a. Diseconomies of scale
b. Productive capacity
c. Marginal physical product
d. Factors of production

19. _____, in microeconomics, are the cost advantages that a business obtains due to expansion. They are factors that cause a producere;s average cost per unit to fall as scale is increased. _____ is a long run concept and refers to reductions in unit cost as the size of a facility, or scale, increases.
a. Isoquant
b. Underinvestment employment relationship
c. Economic production quantity
d. Economies of scale

20. In calculus, a function f defined on a subset of the real numbers with real values is called _____, if for all x and y such that x >≤ y one has f(x) >≤ f(y), so f preserves the order. In layman's terms, the sign of the slope is always positive (the curve tending upwards) or zero (i.e., non-decreasing, or asymptotic, or depicted as a horizontal, flat line) Likewise, a function is called monotonically decreasing (non-increasing) if, whenever x >≤ y, then f(x) >≥ f(y), so it reverses the order.
a. 100-year flood
b. 130-30 fund
c. Monotonic
d. 1921 recession

21. In economics, _____ and economies of scale are related terms that describe what happens as the scale of production increases. They are different terms and should not be used interchangeably.

_____ refers to a technical property of production that examines changes in output subsequent to a proportional change in all inputs (where all inputs increase by a constant factor.)

a. Constant returns to scale
b. Necessity good
c. Customer equity
d. Returns to scale

22. In microeconomics, _____ is quite simply the conversion of inputs into outputs. It is an economic process that uses resources to create a good or service that is suitable for exchange. This can include manufacturing, storing, shipping, and packaging.
a. Solved
b. MET
c. Red Guards
d. Production

Chapter 8. Long-Run Costs and Output Decisions

23. Competitive market equilibrium is the traditional concept of economic equilibrium, appropriate for the analysis of commodity markets with flexible prices and many traders, and serving as the benchmark of efficiency in economic analysis. It relies crucially on the assumption of a competitive environment where each trader decides upon a quantity that is so small compared to the total quantity traded in the market that their individual transactions have no influence on the prices. Competitive markets are an ideal, a standard that other market structures are evaluated by.

A _____ consists of a vector of prices and an allocation such that given the prices, each trader by maximizing his objective function (profit, preferences) subject to his technological possibilities and resource constraints plans to trade into his part of the proposed allocation, and such that the prices make all net trades compatible with one another ('clear the market') by equating aggregate supply and demand for the commodities which are traded.

a. Market system
c. Partial equilibrium

b. Competitive equilibrium
d. Product-Market Growth Matrix

Chapter 9. Input Demand: The Labor and Land Markets

1. The _____ is the market for securities, where companies and governments can raise longterm funds. It is a market in which money is lent for periods longer than a year. The _____ includes the stock market and the bond market.
    a. Capital market
    b. Performance attribution
    c. Multi-family office
    d. Financial instrument

2. _____ is a term in economics, where demand for one good or service occurs as a result of demand for another. This may occur as the former is a part of production of the second. For example, demand for coal leads to _____ for mining, as coal must be mined for coal to be consumed.
    a. Days Sales Outstanding
    b. Derived demand
    c. Leontief production function
    d. Rate risk

3. _____ is the term denoting either an entrance or changes which are inserted into a system and which activate/modify a process. It is an abstract concept, used in the modeling, system(s) design and system(s) exploitation. It is usually connected with other terms, e.g., _____ field, _____ variable, _____ parameter, _____ value, _____ signal, _____ device and _____ file.
    a. ACEA agreement
    b. ACCRA Cost of Living Index
    c. AD-IA Model
    d. Input

4. _____ is an economic model based on price, utility and quantity in a market. It predicts that in a competitive market, price will function to equalize the quantity demanded by consumers, and the quantity supplied by producers, resulting in an economic equilibrium of price and quantity. The model incorporates other factors changing equilibrium as a shift of demand and/or supply.
    a. Joint demand
    b. Deferred gratification
    c. Rational addiction
    d. Supply and demand

5. Economics:

    - _____,the desire to own something and the ability to pay for it
    - _____ curve,a graphic representation of a _____ schedule
    - _____ deposit, the money in checking accounts
    - _____ pull theory,the theory that inflation occurs when _____ for goods and services exceeds existing supplies
    - _____ schedule,a table that lists the quantity of a good a person will buy it each different price
    - _____ side economics,the school of economics at believes government spending and tax cuts open economy by raising _____

    a. Production
    b. McKesson ' Robbins scandal
    c. Demand
    d. Variability

6. _____ in economics and business is the result of an exchange and from that trade we assign a numerical monetary value to a good, service or asset. If Alice trades Bob 4 apples for an orange, the _____ of an orange is 4 apples. Inversely, the _____ of an apple is 1/4 oranges.
    a. Premium pricing
    b. Price war
    c. Price book
    d. Price

Chapter 9. Input Demand: The Labor and Land Markets

7. A _____ is a theoretical term that economists use to describe a market which is free from government intervention (i.e. no regulation, no subsidization, no single monetary system and no governmental monopolies.) In a _____, property rights are voluntarily exchanged at a price arranged solely by the mutual consent of sellers and buyers. By definition, buyers and sellers do not coerce each other, in the sense that they obtain each other's property without the use of physical force, threat of physical force, or fraud, nor is the coerced by a third party (such as by government via transfer payments) and they engage in trade simply because they both consent and believe that it is a good enough choice.
   a. Leninism
   b. Free market
   c. Delegation
   d. Third camp

8. _____ in economics refers to metrics and measures of output from production processes, per unit of input. Labor _____, for example, is typically measured as a ratio of output per labor-hour, an input. _____ may be conceived of as a metrics of the technical or engineering efficiency of production.
   a. Fordism
   b. Production-possibility frontier
   c. Productivity
   d. Piece work

9. CÄ"terÄ«s paribus is a Latin phrase, literally translated as 'with other things the same.' It is commonly rendered in English as 'all other things being equal.' A prediction, or a statement about causal or logical connections between two states of affairs, is qualified by _____ in order to acknowledge, and to rule out, the possibility of other factors which could override the relationship between the antecedent and the consequent.

   A _____ assumption is often fundamental to the predictive purpose of scientific inquiry. In order to formulate scientific laws, it is usually necessary to rule out factors which interfere with examining a specific causal relationship.

   a. Friedman-Savage utility function
   b. Capital outflow
   c. Dematerialization
   d. Ceteris paribus

10. In economics, _____ refers to how the marginal contribution of a factor of production usually decreases as more of the factor is used. According to this relationship, in a production system with fixed and variable inputs, beyond some point, each additional unit of the variable input yields smaller and smaller increases in output. Conversely, producing one more unit of output costs more and more in variable inputs.
    a. Patent troll
    b. Community property
    c. Derivatives law
    d. Diminishing returns

11. In economics, the _____ or marginal physical product is the extra output produced by one more unit of an input (for instance, the difference in output when a firm's labour is increased from five to six units.) Assuming that no other inputs to production change, the _____ of a given input (X) can be expressed as:

    _____ = $\Delta Y/\Delta X$ = (the change of Y)/(the change of X.)

    -
      -
        - Pending approval by Thomas Sowell***

In neoclassical economics, this is the mathematical derivative of the production function.... Note that the 'product' (Y) is typically defined ignoring external costs and benefits.

Chapter 9. Input Demand: The Labor and Land Markets

a. Labor problem
c. Productive capacity
b. Marginal product
d. Factor prices

12. In economics, the _____ also known as MPL or MPN is the change in output from hiring one additional unit of labor. It is the increase in output added by the last unit of labor. Assuming that no other inputs to production change, the marginal product of a given input (X) can be expressed as:

MP = ΔY/ΔX = (the change of Y)/(the change of X.)

a. Marginal product
c. Production function
b. Marginal product of labor
d. Product Pipeline

13. In microeconomics, _____ is the extra revenue that an additional unit of product will bring. It is the additional income from selling one more unit of a good; sometimes equal to price. It can also be described as the change in total revenue/change in number of units sold.

a. Market demand schedule
c. Reservation price
b. Marginal revenue
d. Long term

14. The marginal revenue productivity theory of wages, also referred to as the _____ of labor, is the change in total revenue earned by a firm that results from employing one more unit of labor. It is a neoclassical model that determines, under some conditions, the optimal number of workers to employ at an exogenously determined market wage rate.

The _____ of a worker is equal to the product of the marginal product of labor (MP) and the marginal revenue (MR), given by MR×MP = _____.

a. Coal depletion
c. Marginal revenue product
b. Real prices and ideal prices
d. Marginal revenue productivity theory of wages

15. In microeconomics, _____ is quite simply the conversion of inputs into outputs. It is an economic process that uses resources to create a good or service that is suitable for exchange. This can include manufacturing, storing, shipping, and packaging.

a. Solved
c. MET
b. Production
d. Red Guards

16. In economics and finance, _____ is the change in total cost that arises when the quantity produced changes by one unit. It is the cost of producing one more unit of a good. Mathematically, the _____ function is expressed as the first derivative of the total cost (TC) function with respect to quantity (Q.)

a. Marginal cost
c. Variable cost
b. Khozraschyot
d. Quality costs

17. _____ or economic opportunity loss is the value of the next best alternative foregone as the result of making a decision. _____ analysis is an important part of a company's decision-making processes but is not treated as an actual cost in any financial statement. The next best thing that a person can engage in is referred to as the _____ of doing the best thing and ignoring the next best thing to be done.

a. Economic ideology
b. Economic
c. Industrial organization
d. Opportunity cost

18. In economics, _____ is the process by which a firm determines the price and output level that returns the greatest profit. There are several approaches to this problem. The total revenue--total cost method relies on the fact that profit equals revenue minus cost, and the marginal revenue--marginal cost method is based on the fact that total profit in a perfectly competitive market reaches its maximum point where marginal revenue equals marginal cost.
a. 100-year flood
b. Normal profit
c. Profit margin
d. Profit maximization

19. In management accounting, _____ establishes budget and actual cost of operations, processes, departments or product and the analysis of variances, profitability or social use of funds. Managers use _____ to support decision-making to cut a company's costs and improve profitability. As a form of management accounting, _____ need not follow standards such as GAAP, because its primary use is for internal managers, rather than outside users, and what to compute is instead decided pragmatically.
a. Khozraschyot
b. Cost accounting
c. Total absorption costing
d. Quality costs

20. _____ are the prices that the factors of production of a finished item attract.

There has been some economic debate as to what determines these prices. Classical and Marxist economists argued that the _____ decided the value of a product and so value was intrinsic within the product.

a. Marginal product of labor
b. Factor prices
c. Productivity model
d. Marginal product

21. In economics, _____ are the resources employed to produce goods and services. They facilitate production but do not become part of the product (as with raw materials) or significantly transformed by the production process (as with fuel used to power machinery.) To 19th century economists, the _____ were land (natural resources, gifts from nature), labor (the ability to work), and capital goods (human-made tools and equipment.)
a. Hicks-neutral technical change
b. Product Pipeline
c. Long-run
d. Factors of production

22. Economic _____ is defined as an excess distribution to any factor in a production process above that which is required to induce the factor into the process or any excess above that which is necessary to keep the factor in its current use..

Classical Factor _____ is primarily concerned with the fee paid for the use of fixed (e.g. natural) resources. The classical definition is expressed as any excess payment above that required to induce or provide for production.

a. Rent
b. 130-30 fund
c. 100-year flood
d. 1921 recession

Chapter 9. Input Demand: The Labor and Land Markets

23. In economics, _____ is a measure of the relative satisfaction from consumption of various goods and services. Given this measure, one may speak meaningfully of increasing or decreasing _____, and thereby explain economic behavior in terms of attempts to increase one's _____. For illustrative purposes, changes in _____ are sometimes expressed in units called utils.
   a. Ordinal utility
   b. Expected utility hypothesis
   c. Utility function
   d. Utility

24. _____ is the a method of technical and economic research of the systems for purpose to optimize a parity between system's consumer functions or properties and expenses to achieve those functions or properties.

This methodology for continuous perfection of production, industrial technologies, organizational structures was developed by Juryj Sobolev in 1948 at the 'Perm telephone factory'

- 1948 Juryj Sobolev - the first success in application of a method analysis at the 'Perm telephone factory'.
- 1949 - the first application for the invention as result of use of the new method.

Today in economically developed countries practically each enterprise or the company use methodology of the kind of functional-cost analysis as a practice of the quality management, most full satisfying to principles of standards of series ISO 9000.

- Interest of consumer not in products itself, but the advantage which it will receive from its usage.
- The consumer aspires to reduce his expenses
- Functions needed by consumer can be executed in the various ways, and, hence, with various efficiency and expenses. Among possible alternatives of realization of functions exist such in which the parity of quality and the price is the optimal for the consumer.

The goal of _____ is achievement of the highest consumer satisfaction of production at simultaneous decrease in all kinds of industrial expenses Classical _____ has three English synonyms - Value Engineering, Value Management, Value Analysis.

   a. Staple financing
   b. Monopoly wage
   c. Willingness to pay
   d. Function cost analysis

25. In economics, the _____ can be defined as the graph depicting the relationship between the price of a certain commodity, and the amount of it that consumers are willing and able to purchase at that given price. It is a graphic representation of a demand schedule. The _____ for all consumers together follows from the _____ of every individual consumer: the individual demands at each price are added together.
   a. Cost curve
   b. Kuznets curve
   c. Wage curve
   d. Demand curve

26. _____ is used to assign the available resources in an economic way. It is part of resource management.

In strategic planning, is a plan for using available resources, for example human resources, especially in the near term, to achieve goals for the future.

a. 130-30 fund
b. 100-year flood
c. 1921 recession
d. Resource allocation

27. _____ is a term that is used to describe the overall process of invention, innovation and diffusion of technology or processes. The term is redundant with technological development, technological achievement, and technological progress. In essence _____ is the invention of a technology (or a process), the continuous process of improving a technology (in which it often becomes cheaper) and its diffusion throughout industry or society.
   a. 130-30 fund
   b. 100-year flood
   c. 1921 recession
   d. Technological change

28. The _____ is 'the basic residential unit in which economic production, consumption, inheritance, child rearing, and shelter are organized and carried out'; [the _____] 'may or may not be synonymous with family'.

The _____ is the basic unit of analysis in many social, microeconomic and government models. The term refers to all individuals who live in the same dwelling.

   a. 130-30 fund
   b. 100-year flood
   c. Household
   d. Family economics

29. In economics, _____ is how a natione;s total economy is distributed among its population. ._____ has always been a central concern of economic theory and economic policy. Classical economists such as Adam Smith, Thomas Malthus and David Ricardo were mainly concerned with factor _____, that is, the distribution of income between the main factors of production, land, labour and capital.
   a. Equipment trust certificate
   b. Income Distribution
   c. Authorised capital
   d. Eco commerce

30. To _____ is to impose a financial charge or other levy upon a taxpayer by a state or the functional equivalent of a state.

_____es are also imposed by many subnational entities. _____es consist of direct _____ or indirect _____, and may be paid in money or as its labour equivalent (often but not always unpaid.)

   a. 1921 recession
   b. 100-year flood
   c. 130-30 fund
   d. Tax

Chapter 10. Input Demand: The Capital Market and the Investment Decision

1. _____ refers to the stock of skills and knowledge embodied in the ability to perform labor so as to produce economic value. It is the skills and knowledge gained by a worker through education and experience. Many early economic theories refer to it simply as labor, one of three factors of production, and consider it to be a fungible resource -- homogeneous and easily interchangeable. Other conceptions of labor dispense with these assumptions.

    a. Price theory
    b. Human capital
    c. Law of increasing costs
    d. General equilibrium

2. In general _____ refers to any non-human asset made by humans and then used in production. Often, it refers to economic capital in some ambiguous combination of infrastructural capital and natural capital. As these are combined in process-specific and firm-specific ways that neoclassical macroeconomics does not differentiate at its level of analysis, it is common to refer only to physical vs. human capital and seek so-called 'balanced growth' that develops both in tandem

    Such analyses, however, fails to make distinctions considered critical by many modern economists.

    a. Net domestic product
    b. Linkage principle
    c. Factor cost
    d. Physical capital

3. _____ is a social science concept used in business, economics, organizational behaviour, political science, public health and sociology that refers to connections within and between social networks. Though there are a variety of related definitions, which have been described as 'something of a cure-all' for the problems of modern society, they tend to share the core idea 'that social networks have value. Just as a screwdriver (physical capital) or a college education (human capital) can increase productivity (both individual and collective), so do social contacts affect the productivity of individuals and groups'.

    a. Social inequality
    b. Pre-industrial society
    c. Diversity training
    d. Social capital

4. In finance, a _____ is a debt security, in which the authorized issuer owes the holders a debt and, depending on the terms of the _____, is obliged to pay interest (the coupon) and/or to repay the principal at a later date, termed maturity. A _____ is a formal contract to repay borrowed money with interest at fixed intervals.

    Thus a _____ is like a loan: the issuer is the borrower (debtor), the holder is the lender (creditor), and the coupon is the interest.

    a. Prize Bond
    b. Zero-coupon
    c. Bond
    d. Callable

5. The _____ is the market for securities, where companies and governments can raise longterm funds. It is a market in which money is lent for periods longer than a year. The _____ includes the stock market and the bond market.

    a. Capital market
    b. Multi-family office
    c. Performance attribution
    d. Financial instrument

6. _____ is a term used in accounting, economics and finance to spread the cost of an asset over the span of several years.

    In simple words we can say that _____ is the reduction in the value of an asset due to usage, passage of time, wear and tear, technological outdating or obsolescence, depletion, inadequacy, rot, rust, decay or other such factors.

Chapter 10. Input Demand: The Capital Market and the Investment Decision

In accounting, _____ is a term used to describe any method of attributing the historical or purchase cost of an asset across its useful life, roughly corresponding to normal wear and tear.

a. Depreciation
b. Net income per employee
c. Historical cost
d. Salvage value

7. An _____ is a person who has possession of an enterprise and assumes significant accountability for the inherent risks and the outcome. It is an ambitious leader who combines land, labor, and capital to create and market new goods or services. The term is a loanword from French and was first defined by the Irish economist Richard Cantillon.

a. Expansionary policies
b. ACCRA Cost of Living Index
c. ACEA agreement
d. Entrepreneur

8. To _____ is to impose a financial charge or other levy upon a taxpayer by a state or the functional equivalent of a state.

_____es are also imposed by many subnational entities. _____es consist of direct _____ or indirect _____, and may be paid in money or as its labour equivalent (often but not always unpaid.)

a. 130-30 fund
b. 100-year flood
c. 1921 recession
d. Tax

9. _____ is a fee paid on borrowed assets. It is the price paid for the use of borrowed money, or, money earned by deposited funds. Assets that are sometimes lent with _____ include money, shares, consumer goods through hire purchase, major assets such as aircraft, and even entire factories in finance lease arrangements.

a. Asset protection
b. Internal debt
c. Interest
d. Insolvency

10. An _____ is the price a borrower pays for the use of money they do not own, for instance a small company might borrow from a bank to kick start their business, and the return a lender receives for deferring the use of funds, by lending it to the borrower. _____s are normally expressed as a percentage rate over the period of one year.

_____s targets are also a vital tool of monetary policy and are used to control variables like investment, inflation, and unemployment.

a. Arrow-Debreu model
b. ACCRA Cost of Living Index
c. Interest rate
d. Enterprise value

11. _____ is the difference between price and the costs of bringing to market whatever it is that is accounted as an enterprise (whether by harvest, extraction, manufacture, or purchase) in terms of the component costs of delivered goods and/or services and any operating or other expenses.

A key difficulty in measuring profit is in defining costs. Pure economic monetary profits can be zero or negative even in competitive equilibrium when accounted monetized costs exceed monetized price.

Chapter 10. Input Demand: The Capital Market and the Investment Decision

a. Operating profit
b. Economic profit
c. ACCRA Cost of Living Index
d. Accounting Profit

12. _____ is a type of private equity capital typically provided to early-stage, high-potential, growth companies in the interest of generating a return through an eventual realization event such as an IPO or trade sale of the company. _____ investments are generally made as cash in exchange for shares in the invested company. It is typical for _____ investors to identify and back companies in high technology industries such as biotechnology and ICT.

a. Venture capital
b. Club deal
c. Startup company
d. Collateralized Fund Obligation

13. In economics, a _____ is a mechanism that allows people to easily buy and sell (trade) financial securities (such as stocks and bonds), commodities (such as precious metals or agricultural goods), and other fungible items of value at low transaction costs and at prices that reflect the efficient-market hypothesis.

_____s have evolved significantly over several hundred years and are undergoing constant innovation to improve liquidity.

Both general markets (where many commodities are traded) and specialized markets (where only one commodity is traded) exist.

a. Noise trader
b. Convertible arbitrage
c. Market anomaly
d. Financial Market

14. _____ is a specific term used in companies' financial reporting from the company-whole point of view. Because that use excludes the effects of changing ownership interest, an economic measure of _____ is necessary for financial analysis from the shareholders' point of view

_____ is defined by the Financial Accounting Standards Board, or FASB, as e;the change in equity [net assets] of a business enterprise during a period from transactions and other events and circumstances from nonowner sources. It includes all changes in equity during a period except those resulting from investments by owners and distributions to owners.e;

_____ is the sum of net income and other items that must bypass the income statement because they have not been realized, including items like an unrealized holding gain or loss from available for sale securities and foreign currency translation gains or losses.

a. Comprehensive income
b. Windfall gain
c. Net national income
d. Real income

15. A _____ is a public market for the trading of company stock and derivatives at an agreed price; these are securities listed on a stock exchange as well as those only traded privately.

The size of the world _____ was estimated at about $36.6 trillion US at the beginning of October 2008 . The total world derivatives market has been estimated at about $791 trillion face or nominal value, 11 times the size of the entire world economy.

Chapter 10. Input Demand: The Capital Market and the Investment Decision

a. Adolf Hitler
c. Adam Smith
b. Adolph Fischer
d. Stock market

16. A venture capitalist is a person or investment firm that makes venture investments, and these venture capitalists are expected to bring managerial and technical expertise as well as capital to their investments. A _____ refers to a pooled investment vehicle that primarily invests the financial capital of third-party investors in enterprises that are too risky for the standard capital markets or bank loans.

Venture capital is also associated with job creation, the knowledge economy and used as a proxy measure of innovation within an economic sector or geography.

a. Venture capitalist
c. Venture capital fund
b. Club deal
d. Growth capital

17. _____ is used to assign the available resources in an economic way. It is part of resource management.

In strategic planning,is a plan for using available resources, for example human resources, especially in the near term, to achieve goals for the future.

a. 130-30 fund
c. 1921 recession
b. 100-year flood
d. Resource allocation

18. Economics:

- _____,the desire to own something and the ability to pay for it
- _____ curve,a graphic representation of a _____ schedule
- _____ deposit, the money in checking accounts
- _____ pull theory,the theory that inflation occurs when _____ for goods and services exceeds existing supplies
- _____ schedule,a table that lists the quantity of a good a person will buy it each different price
- _____ side economics,the school of economics at believes government spending and tax cuts open economy by raising _____

a. Demand
c. McKesson ' Robbins scandal
b. Variability
d. Production

19. The _____ is the weighted-average most likely outcome in gambling, probability theory, economics or finance.

What Does _____ Mean? The average of a probability distribution of possible returns, calculated by using the following formula:

E(R)= Sum: probability (in scenario i) * the return (in scenario i)

How do you calculate the average of a probability distribution? As denoted by the above formula, simply take the probability of each possible return outcome and multiply it by the return outcome itself. For example, if you knew a given investment had a 50% chance of earning a 10% return, a 25% chance of earning 20% and a 25% chance of earning -10%, the _____ would be equal to 7.5%:

= (0.5) (0.1) + (0.25) (0.2) + (0.25) (-0.1) = 0.075 = 7.5%

Although this is what you expect the return to be, there is no guarantee that it will be the actual return.

   a. ACCRA Cost of Living Index   b. ACEA agreement
   c. Expected return   d. AD-IA Model

20. _____ or economic opportunity loss is the value of the next best alternative foregone as the result of making a decision. _____ analysis is an important part of a company's decision-making processes but is not treated as an actual cost in any financial statement. The next best thing that a person can engage in is referred to as the _____ of doing the best thing and ignoring the next best thing to be done.
   a. Economic ideology   b. Economic
   c. Industrial organization   d. Opportunity cost

21. In management accounting, _____ establishes budget and actual cost of operations, processes, departments or product and the analysis of variances, profitability or social use of funds. Managers use _____ to support decision-making to cut a company's costs and improve profitability. As a form of management accounting, _____ need not follow standards such as GAAP, because its primary use is for internal managers, rather than outside users, and what to compute is instead decided pragmatically.
   a. Cost accounting   b. Khozraschyot
   c. Total absorption costing   d. Quality costs

22. In finance, _____ rate of profit or sometimes just return, is the ratio of money gained or lost on an investment relative to the amount of money invested. The amount of money gained or lost may be referred to as interest, profit/loss, gain/loss, or net income/loss. The money invested may be referred to as the asset, capital, principal, or the cost basis of the investment.
   a. Sortino ratio   b. Cost accrual ratio
   c. Current ratio   d. Rate of return

23. Cæterìs paribus is a Latin phrase, literally translated as 'with other things the same.' It is commonly rendered in English as 'all other things being equal.' A prediction, or a statement about causal or logical connections between two states of affairs, is qualified by _____ in order to acknowledge, and to rule out, the possibility of other factors which could override the relationship between the antecedent and the consequent.

A _____ assumption is often fundamental to the predictive purpose of scientific inquiry. In order to formulate scientific laws, it is usually necessary to rule out factors which interfere with examining a specific causal relationship.

a. Dematerialization
c. Ceteris paribus
b. Friedman-Savage utility function
d. Capital outflow

24. In microeconomics, _____ is the extra revenue that an additional unit of product will bring. It is the additional income from selling one more unit of a good; sometimes equal to price. It can also be described as the change in total revenue/change in number of units sold.

a. Long term
c. Marginal revenue
b. Market demand schedule
d. Reservation price

25. The marginal revenue productivity theory of wages, also referred to as the _____ of labor, is the change in total revenue earned by a firm that results from employing one more unit of labor. It is a neoclassical model that determines, under some conditions, the optimal number of workers to employ at an exogenously determined market wage rate.

The _____ of a worker is equal to the product of the marginal product of labor (MP) and the marginal revenue (MR), given by MR×MP = _____.

a. Marginal revenue productivity theory of wages
c. Real prices and ideal prices
b. Coal depletion
d. Marginal revenue product

26. _____ is the value on a given date of a future payment or series of future payments, discounted to reflect the time value of money and other factors such as investment risk. _____ calculations are widely used in business and economics to provide a means to compare cash flows at different times on a meaningful 'like to like' basis.

Money value fluctuates over time: $100 today are not worth $100 in five years.

a. Present value of costs
c. Tax shield
b. Future value
d. Present value

27. _____ is the a method of technical and economic research of the systems for purpose to optimize a parity between system's consumer functions or properties and expenses to achieve those functions or properties.

This methodology for continuous perfection of production, industrial technologies, organizational structures was developed by Juryj Sobolev in 1948 at the 'Perm telephone factory'

- 1948 Juryj Sobolev - the first success in application of a method analysis at the 'Perm telephone factory' .
- 1949 - the first application for the invention as result of use of the new method.

Chapter 10. Input Demand: The Capital Market and the Investment Decision

Today in economically developed countries practically each enterprise or the company use methodology of the kind of functional-cost analysis as a practice of the quality management, most full satisfying to principles of standards of series ISO 9000.

- Interest of consumer not in products itself, but the advantage which it will receive from its usage.
- The consumer aspires to reduce his expenses
- Functions needed by consumer can be executed in the various ways, and, hence, with various efficiency and expenses. Among possible alternatives of realization of functions exist such in which the parity of quality and the price is the optimal for the consumer.

The goal of _____ is achievement of the highest consumer satisfaction of production at simultaneous decrease in all kinds of industrial expenses Classical _____ has three English synonyms - Value Engineering, Value Management, Value Analysis.

a. Monopoly wage
c. Staple financing
b. Willingness to pay
d. Function cost analysis

Chapter 11. General Equilibrium and the Efficiency of Perfect Competition

1. The _____ is 'the basic residential unit in which economic production, consumption, inheritance, child rearing, and shelter are organized and carried out'; [the _____] 'may or may not be synonomous with family'.

The _____ is the basic unit of analysis in many social, microeconomic and government models. The term refers to all individuals who live in the same dwelling.

   a. 130-30 fund
   b. 100-year flood
   c. Family economics
   d. Household

2. _____ is the term denoting either an entrance or changes which are inserted into a system and which activate/modify a process. It is an abstract concept, used in the modeling, system(s) design and system(s) exploitation. It is usually connected with other terms, e.g., _____ field, _____ variable, _____ parameter, _____ value, _____ signal, _____ device and _____ file.
   a. ACCRA Cost of Living Index
   b. ACEA agreement
   c. AD-IA Model
   d. Input

3. _____s is the social science that studies the production, distribution, and consumption of goods and services. The term _____s comes from the Ancient Greek oá¼°κονομῖα from oá¼¶κος (oikos, 'house') + νǑμος (nomos, 'custom' or 'law'), hence 'rules of the house(hold)'. Current _____ models developed out of the broader field of political economy in the late 19th century, owing to a desire to use an empirical approach more akin to the physical sciences.
   a. Opportunity cost
   b. Inflation
   c. Economic
   d. Energy economics

4. _____ is the concept or idea of fairness in economics, particularly as to taxation or welfare economics.

In welfare economics, _____ may be distinguished from economic efficiency in overall evaluation of social welfare. Although '_____' has broader uses, it may be posed as a counterpart to economic inequality in yielding a 'good' distribution of welfare.

   a. ACEA agreement
   b. AD-IA Model
   c. ACCRA Cost of Living Index
   d. Equity

5. _____ theory is a branch of theoretical economics. It seeks to explain the behavior of supply, demand and prices in a whole economy with several or many markets. It is often assumed that agents are price takers and in that setting two common notions of equilibrium exist: Walrasian (or competitive) equilibrium, and its generalization; a price equilibrium with transfers.
   a. General equilibrium
   b. New Keynesian economics
   c. Human capital
   d. Rational choice theory

6. _____ is a branch of economics that deals with the performance, structure, and behavior of a national or regional economy as a whole. Along with microeconomics, _____ is one of the two most general fields in economics. It is the study of the behavior and decision-making of entire economies.
   a. Tobit model
   b. New Trade Theory
   c. Macroeconomics
   d. Nominal value

Chapter 11. General Equilibrium and the Efficiency of Perfect Competition

7. _____ is a branch of economics that studies how individuals, households and firms and some states make decisions to allocate limited resources, typically in markets where goods or services are being bought and sold. _____ examines how these decisions and behaviours affect the supply and demand for goods and services, which determines prices; and how prices, in turn, determine the supply and demand of goods and services.

Whereas macroeconomics involves the 'sum total of economic activity, dealing with the issues of growth, inflation and unemployment, and with national economic policies relating to these issues' and the effects of government actions on them.

   a. Countercyclical
   b. New Keynesian economics
   c. Recession
   d. Microeconomics

8. _____ is the branch of economics that incorporates value judgments (that is, normative judgements) about what the economy ought to be like or what particular policy actions ought to be recommended to achieve a desirable goal. _____ looks at the desirability of certain aspects of the economy. It underlies expressions of support for particular economic policies.
   a. Nanoeconomics
   b. Double bottom line
   c. Broad money
   d. Normative economics

9. A _____ is a type of economic equilibrium, where the clearance on the market of some specific goods is obtained independently from prices and quantities demanded and supplied in other markets. In other words, the prices of all substitutes and complements, as well as income levels of consumers are constant. Here the dynamic process is that prices adjust until supply equals demand.
   a. Market system
   b. Horizontal market
   c. Partial equilibrium
   d. Market depth

10. _____ is the branch of economics that concerns the description and explanation of economic phenomena (Wong, 1987, p. 920.) It focuses on facts and cause-and-effect relationships and includes the development and testing of economics theories.
    a. Regulatory economics
    b. 100-year flood
    c. 130-30 fund
    d. Positive economics

11. The _____ consists of a number of economic theories which describe the nature of the firm, company including its existence, its behaviour, and its relationship with the market.

In simplified terms, the _____ aims to answer these questions:

1. Existence - why do firms emerge, why are not all transactions in the economy mediated over the market?
2. Boundaries - why the boundary between firms and the market is located exactly there? Which transactions are performed internally and which are negotiated on the market?
3. Organization - why are firms structured in such specific way? What is the interplay of formal and informal relationships?

Despite looking simple, these questions are not answered by the established economic theory, which usually views firms as given, and treats them as black boxes without any internal structure.

Chapter 11. General Equilibrium and the Efficiency of Perfect Competition

The First World War period saw a change of emphasis in economic theory away from industry-level analysis which mainly included analysing markets to analysis at the level of the firm, as it became increasingly clear that perfect competition was no longer an adequate model of how firms behaved. Economic theory till then had focussed on trying to understand markets alone and there had been little study on understanding why firms or organisations exist.

a. Technology gap
b. Theory of the firm
c. Khazzoom-Brookes postulate
d. Policy Ineffectiveness Proposition

12. _____ is used to assign the available resources in an economic way. It is part of resource management.

In strategic planning, is a plan for using available resources, for example human resources, especially in the near term, to achieve goals for the future.

a. 100-year flood
b. 1921 recession
c. Resource allocation
d. 130-30 fund

13. _____ is a broad label that refers to any individuals or households that use goods and services generated within the economy. The concept of a _____ is used in different contexts, so that the usage and significance of the term may vary.

Typically when business people and economists talk of _____s they are talking about person as _____, an aggregated commodity item with little individuality other than that expressed in the buy/not-buy decision.

a. 100-year flood
b. 1921 recession
c. Consumer
d. 130-30 fund

14. _____ is a situation in which the limited resources of a firm are allocated in accordance with the wishes of consumers. An allocatively efficient economy produces an 'optimal mix' of commodities. A firm is allocatively efficient when its price is equal to its marginal costs (that is, P = MC) in a perfect market.

a. Economic efficiency
b. ACEA agreement
c. Allocative efficiency
d. ACCRA Cost of Living Index

15. Competitive market equilibrium is the traditional concept of economic equilibrium, appropriate for the analysis of commodity markets with flexible prices and many traders, and serving as the benchmark of efficiency in economic analysis. It relies crucially on the assumption of a competitive environment where each trader decides upon a quantity that is so small compared to the total quantity traded in the market that their individual transactions have no influence on the prices. Competitive markets are an ideal, a standard that other market structures are evaluated by.

Chapter 11. General Equilibrium and the Efficiency of Perfect Competition

A _____ consists of a vector of prices and an allocation such that given the prices, each trader by maximizing his objective function (profit, preferences) subject to his technological possibilities and resource constraints plans to trade into his part of the proposed allocation, and such that the prices make all net trades compatible with one another ('clear the market') by equating aggregate supply and demand for the commodities which are traded.

- a. Product-Market Growth Matrix
- b. Partial equilibrium
- c. Market system
- d. Competitive equilibrium

16. _____ is an important concept in economics with broad applications in game theory, engineering and the social sciences. The term is named after Vilfredo Pareto, an Italian economist who used the concept in his studies of economic efficiency and income distribution. Informally, pareto efficient situations are those in which any change to make any person better off would make someone else worse off.
- a. Matching pennies
- b. Lump of labour
- c. Perfect rationality
- d. Pareto efficiency

17. In neoclassical economics and microeconomics, _____ describes the perfect being a market in which there are many small firms, all producing homogeneous goods. In the short term, such markets are productively inefficient as output will not occur where mc is equal to ac, but allocatively efficient, as output under _____ will always occur where mc is equal to mr, and therefore where mc equals ar. However, in the long term, such markets are both allocatively and productively efficient.
- a. Law of supply
- b. General equilibrium
- c. Co-operative economics
- d. Perfect competition

18. In economics, a _____ exists when a specific individual or enterprise has sufficient control over a particular product or service to determine significantly the terms on which other individuals shall have access to it. Monopolies are thus characterized by a lack of economic competition for the good or service that they provide and a lack of viable substitute goods. The verb 'monopolize' refers to the process by which a firm gains persistently greater market share than what is expected under perfect competition.
- a. 130-30 fund
- b. 1921 recession
- c. 100-year flood
- d. Monopoly

19. In economic theory, _____ is the competitive situation in any market where the conditions necessary for perfect competition are not satisfied. It is a market structure that does not meet the conditions of perfect competition.

Forms of _____ include:

- Monopoly, in which there is only one seller of a good.
- Oligopoly, in which there is a small number of sellers.
- Monopolistic competition, in which there are many sellers producing highly differentiated goods.
- Monopsony, in which there is only one buyer of a good.
- Oligopsony, in which there is a small number of buyers.

There may also be _____ in markets due to buyers or sellers lacking information about prices and the goods being traded.

Chapter 11. General Equilibrium and the Efficiency of Perfect Competition

There may also be _____ due to a time lag in a market.

  a. AD-IA Model
  b. ACEA agreement
  c. Imperfect competition
  d. ACCRA Cost of Living Index

20. In economics, a _____ exists when the production or use of goods and services by the market is not efficient. That is, there exists another outcome where all involved can be made better off. _____s can be viewed as scenarios where individuals' pursuit of pure self-interest leads to results that are not efficient - that can be improved upon from the societal point-of-view.

  a. Financial economics
  b. General equilibrium
  c. Market failure
  d. Fixed exchange rate

21. In economics, _____ is the difference between a company's total revenue and its opportunity costs. It is the increase in wealth that an investor has from making an investment, taking into consideration all costs associated with that investment including the opportunity cost of capital.

Profit is the factor income of the entrepreneur.

  a. Accounting profit
  b. Operating profit
  c. Economic profit
  d. ACCRA Cost of Living Index

22. A _____ is an object whose consumption increases the utility of the consumer, for which the quantity demanded exceeds the quantity supplied at zero price. _____s are usually modeled as having diminishing marginal utility. The first individual purchase has high utility; the second has less.

  a. Pie method
  b. Good
  c. Merit good
  d. Composite good

23. _____ is a common market structure where many competing producers sell products that are differentiated from one another (ie. the products are substitutes, but are not exactly alike.) Many markets are monopolistically competitive, common examples include the markets for restaurants, cereal, clothing, shoes and service industries in large cities.

  a. Financial crisis
  b. Perfect competition
  c. Monopolistic competition
  d. Mathematical economics

24. An _____ is a market form in which a market or industry is dominated by a small number of sellers (oligopolists.) Because there are few participants in this type of market, each oligopolist is aware of the actions of the others. The decisions of one firm influence, and are influenced by, the decisions of other firms.

  a. ACCRA Cost of Living Index
  b. Oligopsony
  c. Oligopoly
  d. ACEA agreement

25. In economics, a _____ is a good that is non-rivaled and non-excludable. This means, respectively, that consumption of the good by one individual does not reduce availability of the good for consumption by others; and that no one can be effectively excluded from using the good. In the real world, there may be no such thing as an absolutely non-rivaled and non-excludable good; but economists think that some goods approximate the concept closely enough for the analysis to be economically useful.

Chapter 11. General Equilibrium and the Efficiency of Perfect Competition

a. Neoclassical synthesis
b. Demand-pull theory
c. Happiness economics
d. Public good

26. _____ are defined as public goods that could be delivered as private goods, but are usually delivered by the government for various reasons, including social policy, and finances from public funds like taxes.

Common examples of public goods include: defense and law enforcement (including the system of property rights), public fireworks, lighthouses, clean air and other environmental goods, and information goods, such as software development, authorship, and invention.

a. Privatizing profits and socializing losses
b. Common property
c. Government monopoly
d. Collective goods

27. A _____ is defined in economics as a good that exhibits these properties:

- Excludable - it is reasonably possible to prevent a class of consumers (e.g. those who have not paid for it) from consuming the good.
- Rivalrous - consumptions by one consumer prevents simultaneous consumption by other consumers. _____s satisfies an individual want while public good satisfies a collective want of the society.

A _____ is the opposite of a public good, as they are almost exclusively made for profit.

An example of the _____ is bread: bread eaten by a given person cannot be consumed by another (rivalry), and it is easy for a baker to refuse to trade a loaf (excludable

a. Private good
b. Pie method
c. Positional goods
d. Demerit good

28. _____ is a term from economics referring to the use of money exchanged by buyers and sellers with an open and understood system of value and time trade offs to produce the best distribution of goods and services. The use of the _____ does not imply a free market: there can be captive or controlled markets which seek to use supply and demand, or some other form of charging for scarcity, both in social situations and in engineering.

The _____ assumes perfect competition and is regulated by demand and supply.

a. Two-sided markets
b. Market mechanism
c. Product-Market Growth Matrix
d. Partial equilibrium

Chapter 12. Monopoly and Antitrust Policy

1. In economic theory, _____ is the competitive situation in any market where the conditions necessary for perfect competition are not satisfied. It is a market structure that does not meet the conditions of perfect competition.

Forms of _____ include:

- Monopoly, in which there is only one seller of a good.
- Oligopoly, in which there is a small number of sellers.
- Monopolistic competition, in which there are many sellers producing highly differentiated goods.
- Monopsony, in which there is only one buyer of a good.
- Oligopsony, in which there is a small number of buyers.

There may also be _____ in markets due to buyers or sellers lacking information about prices and the goods being traded.

There may also be _____ due to a time lag in a market.

 a. Imperfect competition   b. ACCRA Cost of Living Index
 c. AD-IA Model   d. ACEA agreement

2. In economics, _____ is the ability of a firm to alter the market price of a good or service. A firm with _____ can raise prices without losing all customers to competitors.

When a firm has _____ it faces a downward-sloping demand curve.

 a. Pacman conjecture   b. Price makers
 c. Revenue-cap regulation   d. Market power

3. In neoclassical economics and microeconomics, _____ describes the perfect being a market in which there are many small firms, all producing homogeneous goods. In the short term, such markets are productively inefficient as output will not occur where mc is equal to ac, but allocatively efficient, as output under _____ will always occur where mc is equal to mr, and therefore where mc equals ar. However, in the long term, such markets are both allocatively and productively efficient.

 a. General equilibrium   b. Perfect competition
 c. Law of supply   d. Co-operative economics

4. In economics, a _____ exists when a specific individual or enterprise has sufficient control over a particular product or service to determine significantly the terms on which other individuals shall have access to it. Monopolies are thus characterized by a lack of economic competition for the good or service that they provide and a lack of viable substitute goods. The verb 'monopolize' refers to the process by which a firm gains persistently greater market share than what is expected under perfect competition.

 a. 100-year flood   b. 130-30 fund
 c. Monopoly   d. 1921 recession

5. In economics and especially in the theory of competition, _____ are obstacles in the path of a firm that make it difficult to enter a given market.

_____ are the source of a firm's pricing power - the ability of a firm to raise prices without losing all its customers.

The term refers to hindrances that an individual may face while trying to gain entrance into a profession or trade.

a. Barriers to entry
b. Limit price
c. Social dumping
d. Group boycott

6. _____ is the public sector analogy to market failure and occurs when a government intervention causes a more inefficient allocation of goods and resources than would occur without that intervention. Likewise, the government's failure to intervene in a market failure that would result in a socially preferable mix of output is referred to as passive _____ (Weimer and Vining, 2004.) Just as with market failures, there are many different kinds of _____s that describe corresponding distortions.

a. Privatizing profits and socializing losses
b. Natural monopoly
c. Government-granted monopoly
d. Government failure

7. _____ is a common market structure where many competing producers sell products that are differentiated from one another (ie. the products are substitutes, but are not exactly alike.) Many markets are monopolistically competitive, common examples include the markets for restaurants, cereal, clothing, shoes and service industries in large cities.

a. Financial crisis
b. Mathematical economics
c. Perfect competition
d. Monopolistic competition

8. An _____ is a market form in which a market or industry is dominated by a small number of sellers (oligopolists.) Because there are few participants in this type of market, each oligopolist is aware of the actions of the others. The decisions of one firm influence, and are influenced by, the decisions of other firms.

a. Oligopoly
b. Oligopsony
c. ACEA agreement
d. ACCRA Cost of Living Index

9. Procter is a surname, and may also refer to:

- Bryan Waller Procter (pseud. Barry Cornwall), English poet
- Goodwin Procter, American law firm
- _____, consumer products multinational

a. Bucket shop
b. Procter ' Gamble
c. Drawdown
d. Tightness

10. In economics, _____ is a measure of the relative satisfaction from consumption of various goods and services. Given this measure, one may speak meaningfully of increasing or decreasing _____, and thereby explain economic behavior in terms of attempts to increase one's _____. For illustrative purposes, changes in _____ are sometimes expressed in units called utils.

a. Utility
b. Utility function
c. Ordinal utility
d. Expected utility hypothesis

Chapter 12. Monopoly and Antitrust Policy

11. A _____ is a set of exclusive rights granted by a state to an inventor or his assignee for a limited period of time in exchange for a disclosure of an invention.

The procedure for granting _____s, the requirements placed on the _____ee and the extent of the exclusive rights vary widely between countries according to national laws and international agreements. Typically, however, a _____ application must include one or more claims defining the invention which must be new, inventive, and useful or industrially applicable.

- a. Bank regulation
- b. Long service leave
- c. Bona fide occupational qualification
- d. Patent

12. _____, in microeconomics, are the cost advantages that a business obtains due to expansion. They are factors that cause a producer;s average cost per unit to fall as scale is increased. _____ is a long run concept and refers to reductions in unit cost as the size of a facility, or scale, increases.

- a. Economic production quantity
- b. Economies of scale
- c. Underinvestment employment relationship
- d. Isoquant

13. In economics, _____ are the resources employed to produce goods and services. They facilitate production but do not become part of the product (as with raw materials) or significantly transformed by the production process (as with fuel used to power machinery.) To 19th century economists, the _____ were land (natural resources, gifts from nature), labor (the ability to work), and capital goods (human-made tools and equipment.)

- a. Hicks-neutral technical change
- b. Long-run
- c. Product Pipeline
- d. Factors of production

14. The _____ is an independent agency of the United States government, established in 1914 by the _____ Act. Its principal mission is the promotion of 'consumer protection' and the elimination and prevention of what regulators perceive to be harmfully 'anti-competitive' business practices, such as coercive monopoly.

The _____ Act was one of President Wilson's major acts against trusts.

- a. 1921 recession
- b. 130-30 fund
- c. Federal Trade Commission
- d. 100-year flood

15. _____ in economics and business is the result of an exchange and from that trade we assign a numerical monetary value to a good, service or asset. If Alice trades Bob 4 apples for an orange, the _____ of an orange is 4 apples. Inversely, the _____ of an apple is 1/4 oranges.

- a. Premium pricing
- b. Price book
- c. Price
- d. Price war

16. In microeconomics, _____ is quite simply the conversion of inputs into outputs. It is an economic process that uses resources to create a good or service that is suitable for exchange. This can include manufacturing, storing, shipping, and packaging.

- a. Solved
- b. MET
- c. Red Guards
- d. Production

Chapter 12. Monopoly and Antitrust Policy

17. In economics, a firm is said to reap monopoly profits when a lack of viable market competition allows it to set its prices above the equilibrium price for a good or service without losing profits to competitors. Monopoly profit is a type of economic profit, that is, it is a profit greater than the normal profit that is typical in a perfectly competitive industry. The resulting price is known as the _____.

   a. Gross Dealer Concession   b. Monopoly price
   c. Payment schedule   d. Gross national income

18. In microeconomics, _____ is the extra revenue that an additional unit of product will bring. It is the additional income from selling one more unit of a good; sometimes equal to price. It can also be described as the change in total revenue/change in number of units sold.

   a. Marginal revenue   b. Long term
   c. Reservation price   d. Market demand schedule

19. _____ exists when sales of identical goods or services are transacted at different prices from the same provider. In a theoretical market with perfect information, no transaction costs or prohibition on secondary exchange (or re-selling) to prevent arbitrage, _____ can only be a feature of monopoly and oligopoly markets, where market power can be exercised. Otherwise, the moment the seller tries to sell the same good at different prices, the buyer at the lower price can arbitrage by selling to the consumer buying at the higher price but with a tiny discount.

   a. Transfer pricing   b. Loss leader
   c. Lerner Index   d. Price discrimination

20. _____ is an economic model based on price, utility and quantity in a market. It predicts that in a competitive market, price will function to equalize the quantity demanded by consumers, and the quantity supplied by producers, resulting in an economic equilibrium of price and quantity. The model incorporates other factors changing equilibrium as a shift of demand and/or supply.

   a. Rational addiction   b. Deferred gratification
   c. Joint demand   d. Supply and demand

21. Economics:

- _____, the desire to own something and the ability to pay for it
- _____ curve, a graphic representation of a _____ schedule
- _____ deposit, the money in checking accounts
- _____ pull theory, the theory that inflation occurs when _____ for goods and services exceeds existing supplies
- _____ schedule, a table that lists the quantity of a good a person will buy it each different price
- _____ side economics, the school of economics at believes government spending and tax cuts open economy by raising _____

   a. McKesson ' Robbins scandal   b. Variability
   c. Production   d. Demand

22. In production, returns to scale refers to changes in output subsequent to a proportional change in all inputs (where all inputs increase by a constant factor.) If output increases by that same proportional change then there are _____ If output increases by less than that proportional change, there are decreasing returns to scale (DRS.)

Chapter 12. Monopoly and Antitrust Policy

a. Lexicographic preferences
b. Long term
c. Consumer sovereignty
d. Constant returns to scale

23. In economics, _____ and economies of scale are related terms that describe what happens as the scale of production increases. They are different terms and should not be used interchangeably.

_____ refers to a technical property of production that examines changes in output subsequent to a proportional change in all inputs (where all inputs increase by a constant factor.)

a. Necessity good
b. Returns to scale
c. Constant returns to scale
d. Customer equity

24. A _____ is a group of people who share or are motivated by at least one common issue or interest, or work together on a specific project(s) to achieve a common objective. _____s are also characterised by attempts to share and exercise political and social power and to make decisions on a consensus-driven and egalitarian basis. _____s differ from cooperatives in that they are not necessarily focused upon an economic benefit or saving (but can be that as well.)

a. 100-year flood
b. 130-30 fund
c. 1921 recession
d. Collective

25. _____ are defined as public goods that could be delivered as private goods, but are usually delivered by the government for various reasons, including social policy, and finances from public funds like taxes.

Common examples of public goods include: defense and law enforcement (including the system of property rights), public fireworks, lighthouses, clean air and other environmental goods, and information goods, such as software development, authorship, and invention.

a. Government monopoly
b. Privatizing profits and socializing losses
c. Common property
d. Collective goods

26. _____ is a broad label that refers to any individuals or households that use goods and services generated within the economy. The concept of a _____ is used in different contexts, so that the usage and significance of the term may vary.

Typically when business people and economists talk of _____s they are talking about person as _____, an aggregated commodity item with little individuality other than that expressed in the buy/not-buy decision.

a. 1921 recession
b. 100-year flood
c. 130-30 fund
d. Consumer

27. _____ or economic opportunity loss is the value of the next best alternative foregone as the result of making a decision. _____ analysis is an important part of a company's decision-making processes but is not treated as an actual cost in any financial statement. The next best thing that a person can engage in is referred to as the _____ of doing the best thing and ignoring the next best thing to be done.

a. Economic ideology
b. Industrial organization
c. Economic
d. Opportunity cost

28. In economics _____ is defined as the sum of private and external costs. Economic theorists ascribe individual decision-making to a calculation costs and benefits. Rational choice theory assumes that individuals only consider their own private costs when making decisions, not the costs that may be borne by others.
    a. Cost-Volume-Profit Analysis
    b. Khozraschyot
    c. Psychic cost
    d. Social cost

29. _____ is an agreement, usually secretive, which occurs between two or more persons to deceive, mislead or to obtain an objective forbidden by law typically involving fraud or gaining an unfair advantage. It is an agreement among firms to divide the market, set prices kickbacks, or misrepresenting the independence of the relationship between the colluding parties.' All acts effected by _____ are considered void.
    a. Dividing territories
    b. Net Book Agreement
    c. Bid rigging
    d. Collusion

30. In management accounting, _____ establishes budget and actual cost of operations, processes, departments or product and the analysis of variances, profitability or social use of funds. Managers use _____ to support decision-making to cut a company's costs and improve profitability. As a form of management accounting, _____ need not follow standards such as GAAP, because its primary use is for internal managers, rather than outside users, and what to compute is instead decided pragmatically.
    a. Quality costs
    b. Total absorption costing
    c. Khozraschyot
    d. Cost accounting

31. A _____ is an object whose consumption increases the utility of the consumer, for which the quantity demanded exceeds the quantity supplied at zero price. _____s are usually modeled as having diminishing marginal utility. The first individual purchase has high utility; the second has less.
    a. Merit good
    b. Composite good
    c. Pie method
    d. Good

32. In 1940, President Franklin Roosevelt split the authority into two agencies, the Civil Aeronautics Administration (CAA) and the _____ The CAA was responsible for air traffic control, safety programs, and airway development. The _____ was entrusted with safety rulemaking, accident investigation, and economic regulation of the airlines.
    a. 1921 recession
    b. 100-year flood
    c. Civil Aeronautics Board
    d. 130-30 fund

33. A _____ is a duty imposed on goods when they are moved across a political boundary. They are usually associated with protectionism, the economic policy of restraining trade between nations. For political reasons, _____s are usually imposed on imported goods, although they may also be imposed on exported goods.
    a. 1921 recession
    b. 130-30 fund
    c. 100-year flood
    d. Tariff

34. _____ in economic theory is the use of modern economic tools to study problems that are traditionally in the province of political science.

Chapter 12. Monopoly and Antitrust Policy

In particular, it studies the behavior of politicians and government officials as mostly self-interested agents and their interactions in the social system either as such or under alternative constitutional rules. These can be represented a number of ways, including standard constrained utility maximization, game theory, or decision theory.

a. Paradox of voting
b. Public choice
c. Public interest theory
d. Rational ignorance

35. Competition law, known in the United States as _____ law, has three main elements:

- prohibiting agreements or practices that restrict free trading and competition between business entities. This includes in particular the repression of cartels.
- banning abusive behaviour by a firm dominating a market, or anti-competitive practices that tend to lead to such a dominant position. Practices controlled in this way may include predatory pricing, tying, price gouging, refusal to deal, and many others.
- supervising the mergers and acquisitions of large corporations, including some joint ventures. Transactions that are considered to threaten the competitive process can be prohibited altogether, or approved subject to 'remedies' such as an obligation to divest part of the merged business or to offer licences or access to facilities to enable other businesses to continue competing.

The substance and practice of competition law varies from jurisdiction to jurisdiction. Protecting the interests of consumers (consumer welfare) and ensuring that entrepreneurs have an opportunity to compete in the market economy are often treated as important objectives. Competition law is closely connected with law on deregulation of access to markets, state aids and subsidies, the privatisation of state owned assets and the establishment of independent sector regulators. In recent decades, competition law has been viewed as a way to provide better public services.

a. Intellectual property law
b. Antitrust
c. Anti-Inflation Act
d. United Kingdom competition law

36. _____ is a term used to describe large corporations, in either an individual or collective sense. The term first came into use in a symbolic sense subsequent to the American Civil War, particularly after 1880, in connection with the combination movement that began in American business at that time. Organizations that fall into the category of '_____' include ExxonMobil, Wal-Mart, Google, Microsoft, General Motors, Citigroup and Arcelor Mittal.

a. Sole proprietorship
b. First-mover advantage
c. Brainsworking
d. Big business

37. A _____ is a counterfeit agreement among industries. It is an informal organization of producers that agree to coordinate prices and production. _____s usually occur in an oligopolistic industry, where there is a small number of sellers and usually involve homogeneous products.

a. Shill
b. Cartel
c. 100-year flood
d. Shanzhai

38. _____ is the transition of a national economy from monopoly control by groups of large businesses to a free market economy. This change rarely arises naturally, and is generally the result of regulation by a governing body.

Chapter 12. Monopoly and Antitrust Policy

A modern example of _____ is the economic restructuring of Germany after the fall of the Third Reich in 1945.

   a. Market power
   b. Complementary monopoly
   c. Monopolization
   d. Decartelization

39. _____ is exchange of capital, goods, and services across international borders or territories. In most countries, it represents a significant share of gross domestic product (GDP.) While _____ has been present throughout much of history , its economic, social, and political importance has been on the rise in recent centuries.
   a. Intra-industry trade
   b. International trade
   c. Import license
   d. Incoterms

40.

The _____ was the first United States Federal statute to limit cartels and monopolies. It falls under antitrust law.

The Act provides: 'Every contract, combination in the form of trust or otherwise, or conspiracy, in restraint of trade or commerce among the several States, or with foreign nations, is declared to be illegal'. The Act also provides: 'Every person who shall monopolize, or attempt to monopolize, or combine or conspire with any other person or persons, to monopolize any part of the trade or commerce among the several States, or with foreign nations, shall be deemed guilty of a felony [. . .]' The Act put responsibility upon government attorneys and district courts to pursue and investigate trusts, companies and organizations suspected of violating the Act. The Clayton Act extended the right to sue under the antitrust laws to 'any person who shall be injured in his business or property by reason of anything forbidden in the antitrust laws.' Under the Clayton Act, private parties may sue in U.S. district court and should they prevail, they may be awarded treble damages and the cost of suit, including reasonable attorney's fees.

   a. 100-year flood
   b. 130-30 fund
   c. 1921 recession
   d. Sherman Antitrust Act

Chapter 12. Monopoly and Antitrust Policy 85

41. A _____ is:

- Rewrite _____, in generative grammar and computer science
- Standardization, a formal and widely-accepted statement, fact, definition, or qualification
- Operation, a determinate _____ for performing a mathematical operation and obtaining a certain result (Mathematics, Logic)
    - Unary operation
    - Binary operation
- _____ of inference, a function from sets of formulae to formulae (Mathematics, Logic)
- _____ of thumb, principle with broad application that is not intended to be strictly accurate or reliable for every situation. Also often simply referred to as a _____
- Moral, an atomic element of a moral code for guiding choices in human behavior
- Heuristic, a quantized '_____' which shows a tendency or probability for successful function
- A regulation, as in sports
- A Production _____, as in computer science
- Procedural law, a _____ set governing the application of laws to cases
    - A law, which may informally be called a '_____'
    - A court ruling, a decision by a court
- In the U.S. Government, a regulation mandated by Congress, but written or expanded upon by the Executive Branch.
- Norm (sociology), an informal but widely accepted _____, concept, truth, definition, or qualification (social norms, legal norms, coding norms)
- Norm (philosophy), a kind of sentence or a reason to act, feel or believe
- 'Rulership' is the concept of governance by a government:
    - Military _____, governance by a military body
    - Monastic _____, a collection of precepts that guides the life of monks or nuns in a religious order where the superior holds the place of Christ
- Slide _____

- '_____,' a song by Ayumi Hamasaki
- '_____,' a song by rapper Nas
- '_____s,' an album by the band The Whitest Boy Alive
- _____s: Pyaar Ka Superhit Formula, a 2003 Bollywood film
- ruler, an instrument for measuring lengths
- _____, a component of an astrolabe, circumferator or similar instrument
- The _____s, a bestselling self-help book
- _____ Project (Run Up-to-date Linux Everywhere), a project that aims to use up-to-date Linux software on old PCs
- _____ engine, a software system that helps managing business _____s
- Ja _____, a hip hop artist
    - R.U.L.E., a 2005 greatest hits album by rapper Ja _____
- '_____s,' a KMFDM song

a. Procter ' Gamble
c. Rule

b. Technocracy
d. Demand

42.

The _____ is a doctrine developed by the United States Supreme Court in its interpretation of the Sherman Antitrust Act. The rule, stated and applied in the case of Standard Oil Co. of New Jersey v. United States, 221 U.S. 1 (1911), is that only combinations and contracts unreasonably restraining trade are subject to actions under the anti-trust laws and that size and possession of monopoly power are not illegal.

a. Negligence in employment
b. Pigford v. Glickman
c. Rule of reason
d. Directive 2006/54/EC

43. _____ was a predominant American integrated oil producing, transporting, refining, and marketing company. Established in 1870 as an Ohio Corporation, it was the largest oil refiner in the world and operated as a major company trust and was one of the world's first and largest multinational corporations until it was broken up by the United States Supreme Court in 1911. John D. Rockefeller was a founder, chairman and major shareholder, and the company made him a billionaire and eventually the richest man in history.

a. 100-year flood
b. Standard Oil
c. 130-30 fund
d. 1921 recession

44. _____ is the prospect that a party insulated from risk may behave differently from the way it would behave if it were fully exposed to the risk. In insurance, _____ that occurs without conscious or malicious action is called morale hazard.

_____ is related to information asymmetry, a situation in which one party in a transaction has more information than another.

a. 1921 recession
b. 130-30 fund
c. Moral hazard
d. 100-year flood

45. The _____ of 1938 is a United States federal law that amended the Federal Trade Commission Act to add the clause 'unfair or deceptive acts or practices in commerce are hereby declared unlawful' to the Section 5 prohibition of unfair methods of competition, in order to protect consumers as well as competition.

1938 amendment to the federal trade commission act that authorized the FTC to restrict unfair or deceptive acts; also called the advertising act. Until this amendment was passed, the FTC could only restrict practices that were unfair to competitors.

a. Fee simple
b. Human rights in Brazil
c. Merger guidelines
d. Wheeler-Lea Act

46. _____, in law, is a term that indicates that a statute permits a court to triple the amount of the actual/compensatory damages to be awarded to a prevailing plaintiff, generally in order to punish the losing party for willful conduct. _____ are a multiple of, and not an addition to, actual damages. Thus, where a person received an award of $100 for an injury, a court applying _____ would raise the award to $300.

a. Personal Responsibility and Work Opportunity Reconciliation Act of 1996
b. Directive 2006/54/EC
c. Property right
d. Treble damages

Chapter 13. Monopolistic Competition and Oligopoly 87

1. _____ is a common market structure where many competing producers sell products that are differentiated from one another (ie. the products are substitutes, but are not exactly alike.) Many markets are monopolistically competitive, common examples include the markets for restaurants, cereal, clothing, shoes and service industries in large cities.
   a. Mathematical economics
   b. Perfect competition
   c. Financial crisis
   d. Monopolistic competition

2. An _____ is a market form in which a market or industry is dominated by a small number of sellers (oligopolists.) Because there are few participants in this type of market, each oligopolist is aware of the actions of the others. The decisions of one firm influence, and are influenced by, the decisions of other firms.
   a. ACCRA Cost of Living Index
   b. Oligopoly
   c. Oligopsony
   d. ACEA agreement

3. In neoclassical economics and microeconomics, _____ describes the perfect being a market in which there are many small firms, all producing homogeneous goods. In the short term, such markets are productively inefficient as output will not occur where mc is equal to ac, but allocatively efficient, as output under _____ will always occur where mc is equal to mr, and therefore where mc equals ar. However, in the long term, such markets are both allocatively and productively efficient.
   a. Law of supply
   b. Co-operative economics
   c. General equilibrium
   d. Perfect competition

4. In economics, a _____ exists when a specific individual or enterprise has sufficient control over a particular product or service to determine significantly the terms on which other individuals shall have access to it. Monopolies are thus characterized by a lack of economic competition for the good or service that they provide and a lack of viable substitute goods. The verb 'monopolize' refers to the process by which a firm gains persistently greater market share than what is expected under perfect competition.
   a. 130-30 fund
   b. 100-year flood
   c. Monopoly
   d. 1921 recession

5. _____ has several particular meanings:

   - in mathematics
     - _____ function
     - Euler _____
     - _____
     - _____ subgroup
     - method of _____s (partial differential equations)
   - in physics and engineering
     - any _____ curve that shows the relationship between certain input- and output parameters, e.g.
     - an I-V or current-voltage _____ is the current in a circuit as a function of the applied voltage
     - Receiver-Operator _____
   - in fiction
     - in Dungeons ' Dragons, _____ is another name for ability score

   a. Characteristic
   b. Technocracy
   c. Demand
   d. Russian financial crisis

Chapter 13. Monopolistic Competition and Oligopoly

6. In marketing, _____ is the process of distinguishing the differences of a product or offering from others, to make it more attractive to a particular target market. This involves differentiating it from competitors' products as well as one's own product offerings.

Differentiation is a source of competitive advantage.

a. Market segment
c. Pricing science
b. Technology acceptance model
d. Product differentiation

7. In coordinate geometry, the _____ is the y-value of the point where the graph of a function or relation intercepts the y-axis of the coordinate system.

In other words, the _____ of a function is the y-value of the point at which it intersects the line x = 0 (the y-axis.) Thus, if the function is specified in form y = f(x), the _____ is easy to find by calculating f.

a. Y-intercept
c. 130-30 fund
b. 100-year flood
d. Ratio

8. Economics:

- _____ ,the desire to own something and the ability to pay for it
- _____ curve, a graphic representation of a _____ schedule
- _____ deposit, the money in checking accounts
- _____ pull theory, the theory that inflation occurs when _____ for goods and services exceeds existing supplies
- _____ schedule, a table that lists the quantity of a good a person will buy it each different price
- _____ side economics, the school of economics at believes government spending and tax cuts open economy by raising _____

a. Variability
c. McKesson ' Robbins scandal
b. Production
d. Demand

9. _____ in economics and business is the result of an exchange and from that trade we assign a numerical monetary value to a good, service or asset. If Alice trades Bob 4 apples for an orange, the _____ of an orange is 4 apples. Inversely, the _____ of an apple is 1/4 oranges.

a. Premium pricing
c. Price book
b. Price war
d. Price

10. In algebra, a _____ is a function depending on n that associates a scalar, det(A), to an n×n square matrix A. The fundamental geometric meaning of a _____ is a scale factor for measure when A is regarded as a linear transformation. _____ s are important both in calculus, where they enter the substitution rule for several variables, and in multilinear algebra.

For a fixed nonnegative integer n, there is a unique _____ function for the n×n matrices over any commutative ring R. In particular, this function exists when R is the field of real or complex numbers.

Chapter 13. Monopolistic Competition and Oligopoly

a. Determinant
c. 1921 recession
b. 130-30 fund
d. 100-year flood

11. In economics, _____ is the ratio of the percent change in one variable to the percent change in another variable. It is a tool for measuring the responsiveness of a function to changes in parameters in a relative way. Commonly analyzed are _____ of substitution, price and wealth.
   a. Elasticity of demand
   c. ACCRA Cost of Living Index
   b. ACEA agreement
   d. Elasticity

12. A _____ is a theoretical term that economists use to describe a market which is free from government intervention (i.e. no regulation, no subsidization, no single monetary system and no governmental monopolies.) In a _____, property rights are voluntarily exchanged at a price arranged solely by the mutual consent of sellers and buyers. By definition, buyers and sellers do not coerce each other, in the sense that they obtain each other's property without the use of physical force, threat of physical force, or fraud, nor is the coerced by a third party (such as by government via transfer payments) and they engage in trade simply because they both consent and believe that it is a good enough choice.
   a. Leninism
   c. Third camp
   b. Delegation
   d. Free market

13. _____s is the social science that studies the production, distribution, and consumption of goods and services. The term _____s comes from the Ancient Greek oá¼°κονομῖα from oá¼¶κος (oikos, 'house') + vÏŒμος (nomos, 'custom' or 'law'), hence 'rules of the house(hold)'. Current _____ models developed out of the broader field of political economy in the late 19th century, owing to a desire to use an empirical approach more akin to the physical sciences.
   a. Economic
   c. Opportunity cost
   b. Energy economics
   d. Inflation

14. _____ is used to refer to a number of related concepts. It is the using resources in such a way as to maximize the production of goods and services. A system can be called economically efficient if:

   - No one can be made better off without making someone else worse off.
   - More output cannot be obtained without increasing the amount of inputs.
   - Production proceeds at the lowest possible per-unit cost.

These definitions of efficiency are not equivalent, but they are all encompassed by the idea that nothing more can be achieved given the resources available.

An economic system is more efficient if it can provide more goods and services for society without using more resources.

   a. Efficient contract theory
   c. ACEA agreement
   b. ACCRA Cost of Living Index
   d. Economic efficiency

15. _____ is used to assign the available resources in an economic way. It is part of resource management.

In strategic planning, is a plan for using available resources, for example human resources, especially in the near term, to achieve goals for the future.

a. 1921 recession
b. 130-30 fund
c. Resource allocation
d. 100-year flood

16. A _____ is a group of people who share or are motivated by at least one common issue or interest, or work together on a specific project(s) to achieve a common objective. _____s are also characterised by attempts to share and exercise political and social power and to make decisions on a consensus-driven and egalitarian basis. _____s differ from cooperatives in that they are not necessarily focused upon an economic benefit or saving (but can be that as well.)

a. 130-30 fund
b. 1921 recession
c. 100-year flood
d. Collective

17. _____ are defined as public goods that could be delivered as private goods, but are usually delivered by the government for various reasons, including social policy, and finances from public funds like taxes.

Common examples of public goods include: defense and law enforcement (including the system of property rights), public fireworks, lighthouses, clean air and other environmental goods, and information goods, such as software development, authorship, and invention.

a. Government monopoly
b. Common property
c. Privatizing profits and socializing losses
d. Collective goods

18. _____ is an agreement, usually secretive, which occurs between two or more persons to deceive, mislead or to obtain an objective forbidden by law typically involving fraud or gaining an unfair advantage. It is an agreement among firms to divide the market, set prices kickbacks, or misrepresenting the independence of the relationship between the colluding parties.' All acts effected by _____ are considered void.

a. Dividing territories
b. Collusion
c. Net Book Agreement
d. Bid rigging

19. A _____ is an object whose consumption increases the utility of the consumer, for which the quantity demanded exceeds the quantity supplied at zero price. _____s are usually modeled as having diminishing marginal utility. The first individual purchase has high utility; the second has less.

a. Good
b. Pie method
c. Merit good
d. Composite good

20. A _____ is a counterfeit agreement among industries. It is an informal organization of producers that agree to coordinate prices and production. _____s usually occur in an oligopolistic industry, where there is a small number of sellers and usually involve homogeneous products.

a. Cartel
b. Shill
c. 100-year flood
d. Shanzhai

21. _____ is the transition of a national economy from monopoly control by groups of large businesses to a free market economy. This change rarely arises naturally, and is generally the result of regulation by a governing body.

A modern example of _____ is the economic restructuring of Germany after the fall of the Third Reich in 1945.

Chapter 13. Monopolistic Competition and Oligopoly 91

    a. Market power
    c. Monopolization
    b. Decartelization
    d. Complementary monopoly

22. _____ is an economic model used to describe an industry structure in which companies compete on the amount of output they will produce, which they decide on independently of each other and at the same time. It is named after Antoine Augustin Cournot (1801-1877) after he observed competition in a spring water duopoly. It has the following features:

- There is more than one firm and all firms produce a homogeneous product, i.e. there is no product differentiation;
- Firms do not cooperate, i.e. there is no collusion;
- Firms have market power, i.e. each firm's output decision affects the good's price;
- The number of firms is fixed;
- Firms compete in quantities, and choose quantities simultaneously;
- The firms are economically rational and act strategically, usually seeking to maximize profit given their competitors' decisions.

An essential assumption of this model is that each firm aims to maximize profits, based on the expectation that its own output decision will not have an effect on the decisions of its rivals. Price is a commonly known decreasing function of total output.

    a. 1921 recession
    c. 130-30 fund
    b. 100-year flood
    d. Cournot competition

23. A true _____ is a specific type of oligopoly where only two producers exist in one market. In reality, this definition is generally used where only two firms have dominant control over a market. In the field of industrial organization, it is the most commonly studied form of oligopoly due to its simplicity.
    a. 100-year flood
    c. Duopoly
    b. Megacorpstate
    d. 130-30 fund

24. The Organization of the Petroleum Exporting Countries is a cartel of twelve countries made up of Algeria, Angola, Ecuador, Iran, Iraq, Kuwait, Libya, Nigeria, Qatar, Saudi Arabia, the United Arab Emirates, and Venezuela. The cartel has maintained its headquarters in Vienna since 1965, and hosts regular meetings among the oil ministers of its Member Countries. Indonesia withdrew its membership in _____ in 2008 after it became a net importer of oil, but stated it would likely return if it became a net exporter in the world.
    a. ACEA agreement
    c. OPEC
    b. AD-IA Model
    d. ACCRA Cost of Living Index

25. _____ is an agreement between business competitors to sell the same product or service at the same price. In general, it is an agreement intended to ultimately push the price of a product as high as possible, leading to profits for all the sellers. _____ can also involve any agreement to fix, peg, discount or stabilize prices.
    a. Price-fixing
    c. Non-price competition
    b. Moral victory
    d. Cut-throat competition

26. _____ occurs when cartels are illegal or overt collusion is absent. Put another way, two firms agree to play a certain strategy without explicitly saying so. This is also known as price leadership, as firms may stay within the law but still tacitly collude by monitoring each other's prices and keeping them the same.

a. Product innovation
b. Poverty penalty
c. Staple port
d. Tacit collusion

27. In economics, the _____ can be defined as the graph depicting the relationship between the price of a certain commodity, and the amount of it that consumers are willing and able to purchase at that given price. It is a graphic representation of a demand schedule. The _____ for all consumers together follows from the _____ of every individual consumer: the individual demands at each price are added together.
   a. Wage curve
   b. Demand curve
   c. Kuznets curve
   d. Cost curve

28. The _____ curve theory is an economic theory regarding oligopoly and monopolistic competition. When it was created, the idea fundamentally challenged classical economic tenets such as efficient markets and rapidly-changing prices, ideas that underly basic supply and demand models. _____ was an initial attempt to explain sticky prices.
   a. Marginal demand
   b. Precautionary demand
   c. Kinked demand curve
   d. Kinked demand

29. The _____ theory is an economic theory regarding oligopoly and monopolistic competition. When it was created, the idea fundamentally challenged classical economic tenets such as efficient markets and rapidly-changing prices, ideas that underly basic supply and demand models. Kinked demand was an initial attempt to explain sticky prices.
   a. Hicksian demand function
   b. Kinked demand
   c. Precautionary demand
   d. Kinked demand curve

30. _____ is a branch of applied mathematics that is used in the social sciences (most notably economics), biology, engineering, political science, international relations, computer science, and philosophy. _____ attempts to mathematically capture behavior in strategic situations, in which an individual's success in making choices depends on the choices of others. While initially developed to analyze competitions in which one individual does better at another's expense (zero sum games), it has been expanded to treat a wide class of interactions, which are classified according to several criteria.
   a. Proper equilibrium
   b. Dollar auction
   c. Discriminatory price auction
   d. Game theory

31. _____ is the practice of selling a product or service at a very low price, intending to drive competitors out of the market, or create barriers to entry for potential new competitors. If competitors or potential competitors cannot sustain equal or lower prices without losing money, they go out of business or choose not to enter the business. The predatory merchant then has fewer competitors or is even a de facto monopoly, and can then raise prices above what the market would otherwise bear.
   a. Restraint of trade
   b. Predatory pricing
   c. Third line forcing
   d. Group boycott

32. _____ is one of the four Ps of the marketing mix. The other three aspects are product, promotion, and place. It is also a key variable in microeconomic price allocation theory.
   a. Point of total assumption
   b. Pricing
   c. Premium pricing
   d. Guaranteed Maximum Price

Chapter 13. Monopolistic Competition and Oligopoly

33. In game theory, _____ is a solution concept of a game involving two or more players, in which each player is assumed to know the equilibrium strategies of the other players, and no player has anything to gain by changing only his or her own strategy unilaterally. If each player has chosen a strategy and no player can benefit by changing his or her strategy while the other players keep theirs unchanged, then the current set of strategy choices and the corresponding payoffs constitute a _____.

Stated simply, Amy and Bill are in _____ if Amy is making the best decision she can, taking into account Bill's decision, and Bill is making the best decision he can, taking into account Amy's decision.

   a. Nash equilibrium
   b. Linear production game
   c. Lump of labour
   d. Proper equilibrium

34. In game theory, a _____ is an extensive form game which consists in some number of repetitions of some base game (called a stage game.) The stage game is usually one of the well-studied 2-person games. It captures the idea that a player will have to take into account the impact of his current action on the future actions of other players; this is sometimes called his reputation.
   a. Repeated game
   b. Quasi-perfect equilibrium
   c. Pursuit-evasion
   d. Correlated equilibrium

35. In economics, a _____ is a market served by only one firm, but with mandated 'competitive' pricing, so as to second the monopoly held by said firm on said market. Its fundamental feature is low barriers to entry and exit; a perfectly _____ would have no barriers to entry or exit. _____s are characteristed by 'hit and run' entry.
   a. Contestable Market
   b. Market mechanism
   c. Horizontal market
   d. Perfect market

36. In economics and especially in the theory of competition, _____ are obstacles in the path of a firm that make it difficult to enter a given market.

_____ are the source of a firm's pricing power - the ability of a firm to raise prices without losing all its customers.

The term refers to hindrances that an individual may face while trying to gain entrance into a profession or trade.

   a. Group boycott
   b. Limit price
   c. Social dumping
   d. Barriers to entry

37. _____ is a term that is used to describe the overall process of invention, innovation and diffusion of technology or processes. The term is redundant with technological development, technological achievement, and technological progress. In essence _____ is the invention of a technology (or a process), the continuous process of improving a technology (in which it often becomes cheaper) and its diffusion throughout industry or society.
   a. 100-year flood
   b. 1921 recession
   c. 130-30 fund
   d. Technological change

Chapter 13. Monopolistic Competition and Oligopoly

38. Competition law, known in the United States as _____ law, has three main elements:

- prohibiting agreements or practices that restrict free trading and competition between business entities. This includes in particular the repression of cartels.
- banning abusive behaviour by a firm dominating a market, or anti-competitive practices that tend to lead to such a dominant position. Practices controlled in this way may include predatory pricing, tying, price gouging, refusal to deal, and many others.
- supervising the mergers and acquisitions of large corporations, including some joint ventures. Transactions that are considered to threaten the competitive process can be prohibited altogether, or approved subject to 'remedies' such as an obligation to divest part of the merged business or to offer licences or access to facilities to enable other businesses to continue competing.

The substance and practice of competition law varies from jurisdiction to jurisdiction. Protecting the interests of consumers (consumer welfare) and ensuring that entrepreneurs have an opportunity to compete in the market economy are often treated as important objectives. Competition law is closely connected with law on deregulation of access to markets, state aids and subsidies, the privatisation of state owned assets and the establishment of independent sector regulators. In recent decades, competition law has been viewed as a way to provide better public services.

    a. Intellectual property law   b. Anti-Inflation Act
    c. Antitrust   d. United Kingdom competition law

39. The Celler-Derek Browne Act is a United States federal law passed in 1950 that reformed and strengthened the Clayton Antitrust Act of 1914 which had amended the Sherman Antitrust Act of 1890. The _____ was passed to close a loophole regarding certain asset acquisitions and acquisitions involving firms that were not direct competitors. While the Clayton Act prohibited stock purchase mergers that resulted in reduced competition, shrewd businessmen were able to find ways around the Clayton Act by simply buying up a competitor's assets.

    a. Patent   b. Celler-Kefauver Act
    c. Civil Rights Act of 1964   d. Leave of absence

40. _____ is the public sector analogy to market failure and occurs when a government intervention causes a more inefficient allocation of goods and resources than would occur without that intervention. Likewise, the government's failure to intervene in a market failure that would result in a socially preferable mix of output is referred to as passive _____ (Weimer and Vining, 2004.) Just as with market failures, there are many different kinds of _____ s that describe corresponding distortions.

    a. Government-granted monopoly   b. Privatizing profits and socializing losses
    c. Natural monopoly   d. Government failure

41. The phrase _____ and acquisitions refers to the aspect of corporate strategy, corporate finance and management dealing with the buying, selling and combining of different companies that can aid, finance, or help a growing company in a given industry grow rapidly without having to create another business entity.

An acquisition, also known as a takeover or a buyout, is the buying of one company (the 'target') by another. An acquisition may be friendly or hostile.

a. Peace dividend
c. Political economy
b. Differential accumulation
d. Mergers

42. In economics, a _____ is the combination of two or more firms competing in the same market with the same good or service. See Horizontal integration.

a. Market dominance
c. Federal Reserve districts
b. Horizontal Merger
d. Financial system

43. The _____ are a set of internal rules promulgated by the Antitrust Division of the United States Department of Justice (DOJ) in conjunction with the Federal Trade Commission (FTC.) These rules, which have been revised a number of times in the past four decades, govern the extent to which these two regulatory bodies will scrutinize and/or challenge a potential merger on grounds of market concentration or threat to competition within a relevant market.

The _____ have sections governing both horizontal integration and vertical integration.

a. Law of increasing relative cost
c. No-FEAR Act
b. Business valuation
d. Merger Guidelines

44. _____ refers to the state of not requiring any outside aid, support for survival; it is therefore a type of personal or collective autonomy. On a large scale, a totally self-sufficient economy that does not trade with the outside world is called an autarky.

The term _____ is usually applied to varieties of sustainable living in which nothing is consumed outside of what is produced by the self-sufficient individuals.

a. Sustainable forest management
c. Sustainability science
b. Self-sufficiency
d. Global Reporting Initiative

Chapter 14. Externalities, Public Goods, Imperfect Information, and Social Choice

1. A _____ is an object whose consumption increases the utility of the consumer, for which the quantity demanded exceeds the quantity supplied at zero price. _____s are usually modeled as having diminishing marginal utility. The first individual purchase has high utility; the second has less.
    a. Pie method
    b. Composite good
    c. Good
    d. Merit good

2. In economics, a _____ exists when the production or use of goods and services by the market is not efficient. That is, there exists another outcome where all involved can be made better off. _____s can be viewed as scenarios where individuals' pursuit of pure self-interest leads to results that are not efficient - that can be improved upon from the societal point-of-view.
    a. Market failure
    b. General equilibrium
    c. Fixed exchange rate
    d. Financial economics

3. In economics, a _____ is a good that is non-rivaled and non-excludable. This means, respectively, that consumption of the good by one individual does not reduce availability of the good for consumption by others; and that no one can be effectively excluded from using the good. In the real world, there may be no such thing as an absolutely non-rivaled and non-excludable good; but economists think that some goods approximate the concept closely enough for the analysis to be economically useful.
    a. Public good
    b. Neoclassical synthesis
    c. Demand-pull theory
    d. Happiness economics

4. _____ are defined as public goods that could be delivered as private goods, but are usually delivered by the government for various reasons, including social policy, and finances from public funds like taxes.

Common examples of public goods include: defense and law enforcement (including the system of property rights), public fireworks, lighthouses, clean air and other environmental goods, and information goods, such as software development, authorship, and invention.

    a. Common property
    b. Government monopoly
    c. Collective goods
    d. Privatizing profits and socializing losses

5. _____ is a broad label that refers to any individuals or households that use goods and services generated within the economy. The concept of a _____ is used in different contexts, so that the usage and significance of the term may vary.

Typically when business people and economists talk of _____s they are talking about person as _____, an aggregated commodity item with little individuality other than that expressed in the buy/not-buy decision.

    a. Consumer
    b. 100-year flood
    c. 1921 recession
    d. 130-30 fund

6. _____s is the social science that studies the production, distribution, and consumption of goods and services. The term _____s comes from the Ancient Greek οἰκονομῖα from οἶκος (oikos, 'house') + νόμος (nomos, 'custom' or 'law'), hence 'rules of the house(hold)'. Current _____ models developed out of the broader field of political economy in the late 19th century, owing to a desire to use an empirical approach more akin to the physical sciences.

Chapter 14. Externalities, Public Goods, Imperfect Information, and Social Choice

a. Economic
b. Energy economics
c. Inflation
d. Opportunity cost

7. _____ is a branch of economics that deals with the performance, structure, and behavior of a national or regional economy as a whole. Along with microeconomics, _____ is one of the two most general fields in economics. It is the study of the behavior and decision-making of entire economies.
   a. Macroeconomics
   b. Tobit model
   c. New Trade Theory
   d. Nominal value

8. In economics and finance, _____ is the change in total cost that arises when the quantity produced changes by one unit. It is the cost of producing one more unit of a good. Mathematically, the _____ function is expressed as the first derivative of the total cost (TC) function with respect to quantity (Q.)
   a. Quality costs
   b. Variable cost
   c. Khozraschyot
   d. Marginal cost

9. _____ is a branch of economics that studies how individuals, households and firms and some states make decisions to allocate limited resources, typically in markets where goods or services are being bought and sold. _____ examines how these decisions and behaviours affect the supply and demand for goods and services, which determines prices; and how prices, in turn, determine the supply and demand of goods and services.

Whereas macroeconomics involves the 'sum total of economic activity, dealing with the issues of growth, inflation and unemployment, and with national economic policies relating to these issues' and the effects of government actions on them.

   a. Microeconomics
   b. Countercyclical
   c. New Keynesian economics
   d. Recession

10. _____ or economic opportunity loss is the value of the next best alternative foregone as the result of making a decision. _____ analysis is an important part of a company's decision-making processes but is not treated as an actual cost in any financial statement. The next best thing that a person can engage in is referred to as the _____ of doing the best thing and ignoring the next best thing to be done.
    a. Economic
    b. Industrial organization
    c. Economic ideology
    d. Opportunity cost

11. _____ is one of the four Ps of the marketing mix. The other three aspects are product, promotion, and place. It is also a key variable in microeconomic price allocation theory.
    a. Premium pricing
    b. Guaranteed Maximum Price
    c. Point of total assumption
    d. Pricing

12. In economics _____ is defined as the sum of private and external costs. Economic theorists ascribe individual decision-making to a calculation costs and benefits. Rational choice theory assumes that individuals only consider their own private costs when making decisions, not the costs that may be borne by others.
    a. Cost-Volume-Profit Analysis
    b. Psychic cost
    c. Social cost
    d. Khozraschyot

Chapter 14. Externalities, Public Goods, Imperfect Information, and Social Choice

13. In management accounting, _____ establishes budget and actual cost of operations, processes, departments or product and the analysis of variances, profitability or social use of funds. Managers use _____ to support decision-making to cut a company's costs and improve profitability. As a form of management accounting, _____ need not follow standards such as GAAP, because its primary use is for internal managers, rather than outside users, and what to compute is instead decided pragmatically.

   a. Khozraschyot   b. Total absorption costing
   c. Quality costs   d. Cost accounting

14. A _____ describes one of a number of pieces of legislation relating to the reduction of smog and air pollution in general. The use by governments to enforce clean air standards has contributed to an improvement in human health and longer life spans. Critics argue it has also sapped corporate profits and contributed to outsourcing, while defenders counter that improved environmental air quality has generated more jobs than it has eliminated.

   a. Smog   b. 130-30 fund
   c. 100-year flood   d. Clean Air Act

15. _____ is an online peer-reviewed magazine published by the Agricultural ' Applied Economics Association (AAEA) for readers interested in the policy and management of agriculture, the food industry, natural resources, rural communities, and the environment. _____ is published quarterly and is available free online. It is currently one of three outreach products offered by AAEA, along with the more timely Policy Issues and the forthcoming Shared Materials section of the AAEA Web site.

   a. 100-year flood   b. 130-30 fund
   c. Choices   d. 1921 recession

16. An _____ is a governmental subsidy paid to farmers and agribusinesses to supplement their income, manage the supply of agricultural commodities, and influence the cost and supply of such commodities. Examples of such commodities include wheat, feed grains (grain used as fodder, such as maize, sorghum, barley, and oats), cotton, milk, rice, peanuts, sugar, tobacco, and oilseeds such as soybeans.

The European Union use agricultural subsidies to encourage self-sufficiency

Agricultural subsidies to European farmers and fisheries make up more than 40 percent of the EU budget.

   a. Agricultural subsidy   b. ACEA agreement
   c. ACCRA Cost of Living Index   d. AD-IA Model

17. To _____ is to impose a financial charge or other levy upon a taxpayer by a state or the functional equivalent of a state.

_____es are also imposed by many subnational entities. _____es consist of direct _____ or indirect _____, and may be paid in money or as its labour equivalent (often but not always unpaid.)

   a. Tax   b. 100-year flood
   c. 1921 recession   d. 130-30 fund

18. To tax is to impose a financial charge or other levy upon a taxpayer by a state or the functional equivalent of a state.

Chapter 14. Externalities, Public Goods, Imperfect Information, and Social Choice

_____ are also imposed by many subnational entities. _____ consist of direct tax or indirect tax, and may be paid in money or as its labour equivalent (often but not always unpaid.)

a. Taxes
b. 1921 recession
c. 130-30 fund
d. 100-year flood

19. In law and economics, the _____, describes the economic efficiency of an economic allocation or outcome in the presence of externalities. The theorem states that when trade in an externality is possible and there are no transaction costs, bargaining will lead to an efficient outcome regardless of the initial allocation of property rights. In practice, obstacles to bargaining or poorly defined property rights can prevent Coasian bargaining.

a. Coase theorem
b. Prior appropriation water rights
c. General Mining Act of 1872
d. Means test

20. In economics, an externality or spillover of an economic transaction is an impact on a party that is not directly involved in the transaction. In such a case, prices do not reflect the full costs or benefits in production or consumption of a product or service. A positive impact is called an _____, while a negative impact is called an external cost.

a. External benefit
b. ACCRA Cost of Living Index
c. AD-IA Model
d. ACEA agreement

21. An _____ is an equitable remedy in the form of a court order, whereby a party is required to do certain acts. The party that fails to adhere to the _____ faces civil or criminal penalties and may have to pay damages or accept sanctions for failing to follow the court's order. In some cases, breaches of _____s are considered serious criminal offences that merit arrest and possible prison sentences.

a. ACCRA Cost of Living Index
b. ACEA agreement
c. AD-IA Model
d. Injunction

22. _____ is the area of law in which manufacturers, distributors, suppliers, retailers, and others who make products available to the public are held responsible for the injuries those products cause.

In the United States, the claims most commonly associated with _____ are negligence, strict liability, breach of warranty, and various consumer protection claims. The majority of _____ laws are determined at the state level and vary widely from state to state.

a. 1921 recession
b. 100-year flood
c. 130-30 fund
d. Product liability

100   *Chapter 14. Externalities, Public Goods, Imperfect Information, and Social Choice*

23. A _____ is:

- Rewrite _____, in generative grammar and computer science
- Standardization, a formal and widely-accepted statement, fact, definition, or qualification
- Operation, a determinate _____ for performing a mathematical operation and obtaining a certain result (Mathematics, Logic)
    - Unary operation
    - Binary operation
- _____ of inference, a function from sets of formulae to formulae (Mathematics, Logic)
- _____ of thumb, principle with broad application that is not intended to be strictly accurate or reliable for every situation. Also often simply referred to as a _____
- Moral, an atomic element of a moral code for guiding choices in human behavior
- Heuristic, a quantized '_____' which shows a tendency or probability for successful function
- A regulation, as in sports
- A Production _____, as in computer science
- Procedural law, a _____ set governing the application of laws to cases
    - A law, which may informally be called a '_____'
    - A court ruling, a decision by a court
- In the U.S. Government, a regulation mandated by Congress, but written or expanded upon by the Executive Branch.
- Norm (sociology), an informal but widely accepted _____, concept, truth, definition, or qualification (social norms, legal norms, coding norms)
- Norm (philosophy), a kind of sentence or a reason to act, feel or believe
- 'Rulership' is the concept of governance by a government:
    - Military _____, governance by a military body
    - Monastic _____, a collection of precepts that guides the life of monks or nuns in a religious order where the superior holds the place of Christ
- Slide _____

- '_____,' a song by Ayumi Hamasaki
- '_____,' a song by rapper Nas
- '_____s,' an album by the band The Whitest Boy Alive
- _____s: Pyaar Ka Superhit Formula, a 2003 Bollywood film
- ruler, an instrument for measuring lengths
- _____, a component of an astrolabe, circumferator or similar instrument
- The _____s, a bestselling self-help book
- _____ Project (Run Up-to-date Linux Everywhere), a project that aims to use up-to-date Linux software on old PCs
- _____ engine, a software system that helps managing business _____s
- Ja _____, a hip hop artist
    - R.U.L.E., a 2005 greatest hits album by rapper Ja _____
- '_____s,' a KMFDM song

a. Rule
b. Procter ' Gamble
c. Demand
d. Technocracy

Chapter 14. Externalities, Public Goods, Imperfect Information, and Social Choice   101

24. _____ is a practice of protecting the environment, on individual, organisational or governmental level, for the benefit of the natural environment and (or) humans.

Due to the pressures of population and technology the biophysical environment is being degraded, sometimes permanently. This has been recognised and governments began placing restraints on activities that caused environmental degradation.

a. ACEA agreement
b. AD-IA Model
c. Environmental Protection
d. ACCRA Cost of Living Index

25. _____ is a common concept in economics, and gives rise to derived concepts such as consumer debt. Generally _____ is defined by opposition to production. But the precise definition can vary because different schools of economists define production quite differently.

a. Consumption
b. Federal Reserve Bank Notes
c. Foreclosure data providers
d. Cash or share options

26. _____ has several particular meanings:

- in mathematics
    - _____ function
    - Euler _____
    - _____
    - _____ subgroup
    - method of _____ s (partial differential equations)
- in physics and engineering
    - any _____ curve that shows the relationship between certain input- and output parameters, e.g.
    - an I-V or current-voltage _____ is the current in a circuit as a function of the applied voltage
    - Receiver-Operator _____
- in fiction
    - in Dungeons ' Dragons, _____ is another name for ability score

a. Technocracy
b. Characteristic
c. Russian financial crisis
d. Demand

27. The _____ is 'the basic residential unit in which economic production, consumption, inheritance, child rearing, and shelter are organized and carried out'; [the _____] 'may or may not be synonomous with family'.

The _____ is the basic unit of analysis in many social, microeconomic and government models. The term refers to all individuals who live in the same dwelling.

a. 130-30 fund
b. 100-year flood
c. Family economics
d. Household

Chapter 14. Externalities, Public Goods, Imperfect Information, and Social Choice

28. In economics, _____ is how a natione;s total economy is distributed among its population. _____ has always been a central concern of economic theory and economic policy. Classical economists such as Adam Smith, Thomas Malthus and David Ricardo were mainly concerned with factor _____, that is, the distribution of income between the main factors of production, land, labour and capital.

   a. Eco commerce
   b. Authorised capital
   c. Equipment trust certificate
   d. Income Distribution

29. A _____ is defined in economics as a good that exhibits these properties:

   - Excludable - it is reasonably possible to prevent a class of consumers (e.g. those who have not paid for it) from consuming the good.
   - Rivalrous - consumptions by one consumer prevents simultaneous consumption by other consumers. _____s satisfies an individual want while public good satisfies a collective want of the society.

   A _____ is the opposite of a public good, as they are almost exclusively made for profit.

   An example of the _____ is bread: bread eaten by a given person cannot be consumed by another (rivalry), and it is easy for a baker to refuse to trade a loaf (excludable

   a. Demerit good
   b. Pie method
   c. Positional goods
   d. Private good

30. Economics:

   - _____,the desire to own something and the ability to pay for it
   - _____ curve,a graphic representation of a _____ schedule
   - _____ deposit, the money in checking accounts
   - _____ pull theory,the theory that inflation occurs when _____ for goods and services exceeds existing supplies
   - _____ schedule,a table that lists the quantity of a good a person will buy it each different price
   - _____ side economics,the school of economics at believes government spending and tax cuts open economy by raising _____

   a. Demand
   b. Production
   c. McKesson ' Robbins scandal
   d. Variability

31. The _____ Tiebout migration is a public choice theory model first described by economist Charles Tiebout in his article 'A Pure Theory of Local Expenditures' The essence of the model is that there is in fact a non-political solution to the free rider problem in local governance.

   Tiebout first proposed the model informally as a graduate student in a seminar with Richard Musgrave, who argued that the free rider problem necessarily required a political solution.

Chapter 14. Externalities, Public Goods, Imperfect Information, and Social Choice

a. 100-year flood
b. 130-30 fund
c. Tiebout model
d. 1921 recession

32. _____, anti-selection insurance, statistics, and risk management. It refers to a market process in which 'bad' results occur when buyers and sellers have asymmetric information (i.e. access to different information): the 'bad' products or customers are more likely to be selected. A bank that sets one price for all its checking account customers runs the risk of being adversely selected against by its low-balance, high-activity (and hence least profitable) customers.
   a. AD-IA Model
   b. Adverse selection
   c. ACCRA Cost of Living Index
   d. ACEA agreement

33. _____ is the prospect that a party insulated from risk may behave differently from the way it would behave if it were fully exposed to the risk. In insurance, _____ that occurs without conscious or malicious action is called morale hazard.

_____ is related to information asymmetry, a situation in which one party in a transaction has more information than another.

   a. 130-30 fund
   b. 1921 recession
   c. 100-year flood
   d. Moral hazard

34. The _____ is an independent agency of the United States government, established in 1914 by the _____ Act. Its principal mission is the promotion of 'consumer protection' and the elimination and prevention of what regulators perceive to be harmfully 'anti-competitive' business practices, such as coercive monopoly.

The _____ Act was one of President Wilson's major acts against trusts.

   a. 100-year flood
   b. 1921 recession
   c. Federal Trade Commission
   d. 130-30 fund

35. _____ is the public sector analogy to market failure and occurs when a government intervention causes a more inefficient allocation of goods and resources than would occur without that intervention. Likewise, the government's failure to intervene in a market failure that would result in a socially preferable mix of output is referred to as passive _____ (Weimer and Vining, 2004.) Just as with market failures, there are many different kinds of _____s that describe corresponding distortions.
   a. Government-granted monopoly
   b. Natural monopoly
   c. Privatizing profits and socializing losses
   d. Government failure

36. Although information has been bought and sold since ancient times, the idea of an information marketplace is relatively recent. The nature of such markets is still evolving, which complicates development of sustainable business models. However, certain attributes of _____ are beginning to be understood, such as diminished participation costs, opportunities for customization, shifting customer relations, and a need for order.
   a. Underground economy
   b. Information markets
   c. Intention economy
   d. Open economy

Chapter 14. Externalities, Public Goods, Imperfect Information, and Social Choice

37. In social choice theory, Arrow's _____ demonstrates that no voting system can convert the ranked preferences of individuals into a community-wide ranking while also meeting a certain set of reasonable criteria with three or more discrete options to choose from. These criteria are called unrestricted domain, non-imposition, non-dictatorship, Pareto efficiency, and independence of irrelevant alternatives. The theorem is often cited in discussions of election theory as it is further interpreted by the Gibbard-Satterthwaite theorem.
   a. ACEA agreement
   b. AD-IA Model
   c. ACCRA Cost of Living Index
   d. Impossibility theorem

38. _____s are American state laws that provide a remedy for purchasers of cars that repeatedly fail to meet standards of quality and performance. These cars are called lemons. The federal _____ protects citizens of all states.
   a. High-reeve
   b. No Child Left Behind
   c. Celler-Kefauver Act
   d. Lemon law

39. _____ studies how measures of individual interests, values, or welfares in theory could be aggregated to reach a collective decision. A non-theoretical example of a collective decision is passing a set of laws under a constitution. _____ dates from Condorcet's formulation of the voting paradox.
   a. Social choice theory
   b. 1921 recession
   c. 100-year flood
   d. 130-30 fund

40. The _____ is a situation noted by the Marquis de Condorcet in the late 18th century, in which collective preferences can be cyclic, even if the preferences of individual voters are not. This is paradoxical, because it means that majority wishes can be in conflict with each other. When this occurs, it is because the conflicting majorities are each made up of different groups of individuals.
   a. 130-30 fund
   b. 1921 recession
   c. 100-year flood
   d. Voting paradox

41. The _____ is the apparent contradiction that although water is on the whole more useful, in terms of survival, than diamonds, diamonds command a higher price in the market. The economist Adam Smith is often considered to be the classic presenter of this paradox. Nicolaus Copernicus, John Locke, John Law and others had previously tried to explain the disparity.
   a. 100-year flood
   b. Paradox of value
   c. 130-30 fund
   d. St. Petersburg paradox

42. _____ is the trading of favors or quid pro quo, such as vote trading by legislative members to obtain passage of actions of interest to each legislative member. It is also the 'cross quoting' of papers by academics in order to drive up reference counts. The Nuttall Encyclopedia describes log-rolling as 'mutual praise by authors of each other's work.' American frontiersman Davy Crockett was one of the first to apply the term to legislation:

The first known use of the term was by Congressman Davy Crockett, who said on the floor (of the U.S. House of Representatives) in 1835, 'my people don't like me to log-roll in their business, and vote away pre-emption rights to fellows in other states that never kindle a fire on their own land.'

The widest accepted origin is the old custom of neighbors assisting each other with the moving of logs.

a. 1921 recession	b. Logrolling
c. 130-30 fund	d. 100-year flood

43. _____ is the incidence or process of transferring ownership of a business, enterprise, agency or public service from the public sector (government) to the private sector (business.) In a broader sense, _____ refers to transfer of any government function to the private sector including governmental functions like revenue collection and law enforcement.

The term '_____' also has been used to describe two unrelated transactions.

a. Ricardian equivalence	b. Compound empowerment
c. Performance reports	d. Privatization

44. _____ in economic theory is the use of modern economic tools to study problems that are traditionally in the province of political science.

In particular, it studies the behavior of politicians and government officials as mostly self-interested agents and their interactions in the social system either as such or under alternative constitutional rules. These can be represented a number of ways, including standard constrained utility maximization, game theory, or decision theory.

a. Public interest theory	b. Paradox of voting
c. Public choice	d. Rational ignorance

Chapter 15. Income Distribution and Poverty

1. _____ is the concept or idea of fairness in economics, particularly as to taxation or welfare economics.

In welfare economics, _____ may be distinguished from economic efficiency in overall evaluation of social welfare. Although '_____' has broader uses, it may be posed as a counterpart to economic inequality in yielding a 'good' distribution of welfare.

    a. AD-IA Model
    c. Equity
    b. ACEA agreement
    d. ACCRA Cost of Living Index

2. In economics, _____ is a measure of the relative satisfaction from consumption of various goods and services. Given this measure, one may speak meaningfully of increasing or decreasing _____, and thereby explain economic behavior in terms of attempts to increase one's _____. For illustrative purposes, changes in _____ are sometimes expressed in units called utils.

    a. Expected utility hypothesis
    c. Utility
    b. Utility function
    d. Ordinal utility

3. The _____ is 'the basic residential unit in which economic production, consumption, inheritance, child rearing, and shelter are organized and carried out'; [the _____] 'may or may not be synonomous with family'.

The _____ is the basic unit of analysis in many social, microeconomic and government models. The term refers to all individuals who live in the same dwelling.

    a. Family economics
    c. 130-30 fund
    b. 100-year flood
    d. Household

4. _____ is a comparison of the wealth of various members or groups in a society. It differs from the distribution of income in a manner analogous to the difference between position and speed.

Wealth is a person's net worth, expressed as:

    wealth = assets - liabilities

The word 'wealth' is often confused with 'income'.

    a. 100-year flood
    c. Wealth condensation
    b. 130-30 fund
    d. Distribution of Wealth

5. In economics, _____ is how a natione;s total economy is distributed among its population. ._____ has always been a central concern of economic theory and economic policy. Classical economists such as Adam Smith, Thomas Malthus and David Ricardo were mainly concerned with factor _____, that is, the distribution of income between the main factors of production, land, labour and capital.

    a. Authorised capital
    c. Equipment trust certificate
    b. Eco commerce
    d. Income Distribution

6. To _____ is to impose a financial charge or other levy upon a taxpayer by a state or the functional equivalent of a state.

Chapter 15. Income Distribution and Poverty

_____es are also imposed by many subnational entities. _____es consist of direct _____ or indirect _____, and may be paid in money or as its labour equivalent (often but not always unpaid.)

- a. 130-30 fund
- b. 100-year flood
- c. Tax
- d. 1921 recession

7. _____ is a term used in labor economics to analyze the relation between the wage rate and the unpleasantness, risk, or other undesirable attributes of a particular job. A _____, which is also called a compensating wage differential or an equalizing difference, is defined as the additional amount of income that a given worker must be offered in order to motivate them to accept a given undesirable job, relative to other jobs that worker could perform. One can also speak of the _____ for an especially desirable job, or one that provides special benefits, but in this case the differential would be negative: that is, a given worker would be willing to accept a lower wage for an especially desirable job, relative to other jobs.

- a. Compensating differential
- b. 100-year flood
- c. Search theory
- d. Wage dispersion

8. _____ refers to the stock of skills and knowledge embodied in the ability to perform labor so as to produce economic value. It is the skills and knowledge gained by a worker through education and experience. Many early economic theories refer to it simply as labor, one of three factors of production, and consider it to be a fungible resource -- homogeneous and easily interchangeable. Other conceptions of labor dispense with these assumptions.

- a. General equilibrium
- b. Human capital
- c. Price theory
- d. Law of increasing costs

9. The _____ of 1938 (_____, ch. 676, 52 Stat. 1060, June 25, 1938, 29 U.S.C.ch.8), also called the Wages and Hours Bill, is United States federal law that applies to employees engaged in interstate commerce or employed by an enterprise engaged in commerce or in the production of goods for commerce, unless the employer can claim an exemption from coverage.

- a. Fair Labor Standards Act
- b. Habitability
- c. Generalized System of Preferences
- d. Hostile work environment

10. A _____ is the lowest hourly, daily or monthly wage that employers may legally pay to employees or workers. Equivalently, it is the lowest wage at which workers may sell their labor. Although _____ laws are in effect in a great many jurisdictions, there are differences of opinion about the benefits and drawbacks of a _____.

- a. Microfoundations
- b. Marginal propensity to consume
- c. Permanent war economy
- d. Minimum wage

11. _____s is the social science that studies the production, distribution, and consumption of goods and services. The term _____s comes from the Ancient Greek oá¼°κονομῖα from oá¼¶κος (oikos, 'house') + νῌμος (nomos, 'custom' or 'law'), hence 'rules of the house(hold)'. Current _____ models developed out of the broader field of political economy in the late 19th century, owing to a desire to use an empirical approach more akin to the physical sciences.

- a. Opportunity cost
- b. Energy economics
- c. Economic
- d. Inflation

Chapter 15. Income Distribution and Poverty

12. _____ is the public sector analogy to market failure and occurs when a government intervention causes a more inefficient allocation of goods and resources than would occur without that intervention. Likewise, the government's failure to intervene in a market failure that would result in a socially preferable mix of output is referred to as passive _____ (Weimer and Vining, 2004.) Just as with market failures, there are many different kinds of _____s that describe corresponding distortions.
   a. Natural monopoly
   b. Privatizing profits and socializing losses
   c. Government failure
   d. Government-granted monopoly

13. In economics, a _____ is a redistribution of income in the market system. These payments are considered to be nonexhaustive because they do not directly absorb resources or create output. Examples of certain _____s include welfare (financial aid), social security, and government subsidies for certain businesses (firms.)
   a. 1921 recession
   b. 100-year flood
   c. 130-30 fund
   d. Transfer payment

14. A _____ is the transfer of wealth from one party (such as a person or company) to another. A _____ is usually made in exchange for the provision of goods, services or both, or to fulfill a legal obligation.

The simplest and oldest form of _____ is barter, the exchange of one good or service for another.

   a. Going concern
   b. Social gravity
   c. Soft count
   d. Payment

15. The _____ is a measure of statistical dispersion, commonly used as a measure of inequality of income distribution or inequality of wealth distribution. It is defined as a ratio with values between 0 and 1: A low _____ indicates more equal income or wealth distribution, while a high _____ indicates more unequal distribution. 0 corresponds to perfect equality (everyone having exactly the same income) and 1 corresponds to perfect inequality (where one person has all the income, while everyone else has zero income.)
   a. Leapfrogging
   b. Compensating variation
   c. Suits index
   d. Gini coefficient

16. In economics, the _____ is a graphical representation of the cumulative distribution function of a probability distribution; it is a graph showing the proportion of the distribution assumed by the bottom y% of the values. It is a curve that illustrates income distribution. It is often used to represent income distribution, where it shows for the bottom x% of households, what percentage y% of the total income they have.
   a. Kuznets curve
   b. Demand curve
   c. Phillips curve
   d. Lorenz curve

17. In mathematics, a _____ is a constant multiplicative factor of a certain object. For example, in the expression $9x^2$, the _____ of x^2 is 9.

The object can be such things as a variable, a vector, a function, etc.

   a. Coefficient
   b. 100-year flood
   c. 1921 recession
   d. 130-30 fund

Chapter 15. Income Distribution and Poverty

18. _____ is the shortage of common things such as food, clothing, shelter and safe drinking water, all of which determine the quality of life. It may also include the lack of access to opportunities such as education and employment which aid the escape from _____ and/or allow one to enjoy the respect of fellow citizens. According to Mollie Orshansky who developed the _____ measurements used by the U.S. government, 'to be poor is to be deprived of those goods and services and pleasures which others around us take for granted.' Ongoing debates over causes, effects and best ways to measure _____, directly influence the design and implementation of _____-reduction programs and are therefore relevant to the fields of public administration and international development.

   a. Liberal welfare reforms
   b. Poverty map
   c. Growth Elasticity of Poverty
   d. Poverty

19. The _____ is the minimum level of income deemed necessary to achieve an adequate standard of living in a given country. In practice, like the definition of poverty, the official or common understanding of the poverty line is significantly higher in developed countries than in developing countries.

The common international poverty line has been roughly $1 a day, or more precisely $1.08 at 1993 purchasing-power parity (PPP.)

   a. Poverty
   b. Poverty map
   c. Poverty reduction
   d. Poverty threshold

20. In mathematics, an _____ is a statement about the relative size or order of two objects, or about whether they are the same or not

   - The notation a < b means that a is less than b.
   - The notation a > b means that a is greater than b.
   - The notation a ≠ b means that a is not equal to b, but does not say that one is greater than the other or even that they can be compared in size.

In each statement above, a is not equal to b. These relations are known as strict inequalities. The notation a < b may also be read as 'a is strictly less than b'.

   a. ACCRA Cost of Living Index
   b. Inequality
   c. AD-IA Model
   d. ACEA agreement

21. In economics, _____ is the transfer of income, wealth or property from some individuals to others.

One premise of _____ is that money should be distributed to benefit the poorer members of society, and that the rich have an obligation to assist the poor, thus creating a more financially egalitarian society. Another argument is that the rich exploit the poor or otherwise gain unfair benefits.

   a. Redistribution
   b. 130-30 fund
   c. 1921 recession
   d. 100-year flood

22. _____: Kritik der politischen Ökonomie is an extensive treatise on political economy written in German by Karl Marx and edited in part by Friedrich Engels. The book is a critical analysis of capitalism. Its first volume was published in 1867.

Chapter 15. Income Distribution and Poverty

a. Das Kapital
b. Dialectics of Nature
c. Capital accumulation
d. Productive force

23. _____ was an English philosopher. Locke is considered the first of the British empiricists, but is equally important to social contract theory. His ideas had enormous influence on the development of epistemology and political philosophy, and he is widely regarded as one of the most influential Enlightenment thinkers, classical republicans, and contributors to liberal theory.

a. 1921 recession
b. 130-30 fund
c. 100-year flood
d. John Locke

24.

_____ was a German philosopher, political economist, historian, political theorist, sociologist, communist and revolutionary credited as the founder of communism.

Marx summarized his approach to history and politics in the opening line of the first chapter of The Communist Manifesto : e;The history of all hitherto existing society is the history of class struggles.e; Marx argued that capitalism, like previous socioeconomic systems, will produce internal tensions which will lead to its destruction. Just as capitalism replaced feudalism, socialism will in its turn replace capitalism and lead to a stateless, classless society which will emerge after a transitional period, the 'dictatorship of the proletariat'.

a. Neo-Gramscianism
b. Karl Heinrich Marx
c. Marxism
d. Adam Smith

25. _____ describes a broad class of theories that try to explain the ways in which people form states and/or maintain social order. The notion of the _____ implies that the people give up some rights to a government or other authority in order to receive or maintain social order.

_____ theory formed a central pillar in the historically important notion that legitimate state authority must be derived from the consent of the governed.

a. Social contract
b. 100-year flood
c. 1921 recession
d. 130-30 fund

26. In economics, _____ studies how economic actors can and do construct contractual arrangements, generally in the presence of asymmetric information. _____ is closely connected to the field of law and economics. One prominent field of application is managerial compensation.

a. Contract theory
b. Buydown
c. Negligence in employment
d. Nexus of contracts

27. The _____ consists of a number of economic theories which describe the nature of the firm, company including its existence, its behaviour, and its relationship with the market.

Chapter 15. Income Distribution and Poverty   111

In simplified terms, the _____ aims to answer these questions:

1. Existence - why do firms emerge, why are not all transactions in the economy mediated over the market?
2. Boundaries - why the boundary between firms and the market is located exactly there? Which transactions are performed internally and which are negotiated on the market?
3. Organization - why are firms structured in such specific way? What is the interplay of formal and informal relationships?

Despite looking simple, these questions are not answered by the established economic theory, which usually views firms as given, and treats them as black boxes without any internal structure.

The First World War period saw a change of emphasis in economic theory away from industry-level analysis which mainly included analysing markets to analysis at the level of the firm, as it became increasingly clear that perfect competition was no longer an adequate model of how firms behaved. Economic theory till then had focussed on trying to understand markets alone and there had been little study on understanding why firms or organisations exist.

- a. Policy Ineffectiveness Proposition
- b. Khazzoom-Brookes postulate
- c. Technology gap
- d. Theory of the firm

28. _____ refers to a tax levied by various jurisdictions on the profits made by companies or associations. It is a tax on the value of the corporation's profits.

The measure of taxable profits varies from country to country.

- a. Business engineering
- b. Captive unit
- c. Business process reengineering
- d. Corporate tax

29. In economics, a _____ is a good that is non-rivaled and non-excludable. This means, respectively, that consumption of the good by one individual does not reduce availability of the good for consumption by others; and that no one can be effectively excluded from using the good. In the real world, there may be no such thing as an absolutely non-rivaled and non-excludable good; but economists think that some goods approximate the concept closely enough for the analysis to be economically useful.
- a. Neoclassical synthesis
- b. Happiness economics
- c. Demand-pull theory
- d. Public good

30. To tax is to impose a financial charge or other levy upon a taxpayer by a state or the functional equivalent of a state.

_____ are also imposed by many subnational entities. _____ consist of direct tax or indirect tax, and may be paid in money or as its labour equivalent (often but not always unpaid.)

- a. 130-30 fund
- b. 100-year flood
- c. 1921 recession
- d. Taxes

Chapter 15. Income Distribution and Poverty

31. A _____ is an object whose consumption increases the utility of the consumer, for which the quantity demanded exceeds the quantity supplied at zero price. _____s are usually modeled as having diminishing marginal utility. The first individual purchase has high utility; the second has less.
   a. Merit good
   b. Pie method
   c. Composite good
   d. Good

32. _____ is the a method of technical and economic research of the systems for purpose to optimize a parity between system's consumer functions or properties and expenses to achieve those functions or properties.

This methodology for continuous perfection of production, industrial technologies, organizational structures was developed by Juryj Sobolev in 1948 at the 'Perm telephone factory'

- 1948 Juryj Sobolev - the first success in application of a method analysis at the 'Perm telephone factory'.
- 1949 - the first application for the invention as result of use of the new method.

Today in economically developed countries practically each enterprise or the company use methodology of the kind of functional-cost analysis as a practice of the quality management, most full satisfying to principles of standards of series ISO 9000.

- Interest of consumer not in products itself, but the advantage which it will receive from its usage.
- The consumer aspires to reduce his expenses
- Functions needed by consumer can be executed in the various ways, and, hence, with various efficiency and expenses. Among possible alternatives of realization of functions exist such in which the parity of quality and the price is the optimal for the consumer.

The goal of _____ is achievement of the highest consumer satisfaction of production at simultaneous decrease in all kinds of industrial expenses Classical _____ has three English synonyms - Value Engineering, Value Management, Value Analysis.

   a. Willingness to pay
   b. Monopoly wage
   c. Staple financing
   d. Function cost analysis

33. _____, often called disability income insurance, is a form of insurance that insures the beneficiary's earned income against the risk that disability will make working (and therefore earning) impossible. It includes paid sick leave, short-term disability benefits, and long-term disability benefits.

In most developed countries, the single most important form of _____ is that provided by the national government for all citizens.

   a. 1921 recession
   b. 130-30 fund
   c. 100-year flood
   d. Disability insurance

34. An _____ is a tax levied on the financial income of people, corporations, or other legal entities. Various _____ systems exist, with varying degrees of tax incidence. Income taxation can be progressive, proportional, or regressive.

Chapter 15. Income Distribution and Poverty

a. ACCRA Cost of Living Index
b. AD-IA Model
c. Income tax
d. ACEA agreement

35. _____, in law and economics, is a form of risk management primarily used to hedge against the risk of a contingent loss. _____ is defined as the equitable transfer of the risk of a loss, from one entity to another, in exchange for a premium, and can be thought of as a guaranteed small loss to prevent a large, possibly devastating loss. An insurer is a company selling the _____; an insured or policyholder is the person or entity buying the _____.

a. ACCRA Cost of Living Index
b. ACEA agreement
c. AD-IA Model
d. Insurance

36. In a company, _____ is the sum of all financial records of salaries, wages, bonuses and deductions.

A paycheck, is traditionally a paper document issued by an employer to pay an employee for services rendered. While most commonly used in the United States, recently the physical paycheck has been increasingly replaced by electronic direct deposit to bank accounts.

a. 100-year flood
b. Tax expense
c. Payroll
d. Total Expense Ratio

37. _____ is the process of changing the way taxes are collected or managed by the government.

_____ers have different goals. Some seek to reduce the level of taxation of all people by the government.

a. Tax Reform
b. Tax break
c. Nil-rate band
d. Special-purpose local-option sales tax

38. _____ is the codified system of laws that describes government levies on economic transactions, commonly called taxes.

Primary taxation issues facing the governments world over include;

- taxes on income and wealth (or estates)
- taxation of capital gains
- taxation of retirement pensions and social security contributions etc.
- inheritance taxes
- taxation of gifts
- consumption taxes (or sales tax)
- taxation of corporations, LLCs, partnerships

In law schools, '_____' is a sub-discipline and area of specialist study. _____ specialists are often employed in consultative roles, and may also be involved in litigation. Many U.S. law schools require about 30 semester credit hours of required courses and approximately 60 hours or more of electives.

a. Tax harmonization
b. Virtual tax
c. Popiwek
d. Tax law

39. _____ is a voluntary transfer of resources from one country to another, given at least partly with the objective of benefiting the recipient country. It may have other functions as well: it may be given as a signal of diplomatic approval, or to strengthen a military ally, to reward a government for behaviour desired by the donor, to extend the donor's cultural influence, to provide infrastructure needed by the donor for resource extraction from the recipient country, or to gain other kinds of commercial access. Humanitarianism and altruism are, nevertheless, significant motivations for the giving of _____.

a. ACCRA Cost of Living Index
b. ACEA agreement
c. Aid
d. AD-IA Model

40. _____ was a federal assistance program in effect from 1935 to 1997, which was administered by the United States Department of Health and Human Services. This program provided financial assistance to children whose families had low or no income.

The program was created under the name Aid to Dependent Children (ADC) by the Social Security Act of 1935 as part of the New Deal; the words 'families with' were added to the name in 1960, partly due to concern that the program's rules discouraged marriage.

a. ACEA agreement
b. ACCRA Cost of Living Index
c. AD-IA Model
d. Aid to Families with Dependent Children

41. _____ is the United States of America's federal assistance program, formerly known as 'welfare'. It began on July 1, 1997, and succeeded the Aid to Families with Dependent Children program, providing cash assistance to indigent American families with dependent children through the United States Department of Health and Human Services. Prior to 1997, the federal government designed the overall program requirements and guidelines, while states administered the program and determined eligibility for benefits.

a. 1921 recession
b. 130-30 fund
c. 100-year flood
d. Temporary Assistance for Needy Families

42. _____ is a form of housing tenure in which the property is owned by a government authority, which may be central or local. Social housing is an umbrella term referring to rental housing which may be owned and managed by the state, by not-for-profit organizations, or by a combination of the two, usually with the aim of providing affordable housing.

Although the common goal of _____ is to provide affordable housing, the details, terminology, definitions of poverty and other criteria for allocation vary.

a. 100-year flood
b. Public Housing
c. 1921 recession
d. 130-30 fund

43. A _____ refers to any type debt instrument, such as a loan, bond, mortgage that does not have a fixed rate of interest over the life of the instrument. Such debt typically uses an index or other base rate for establishing the interest rate for each relevant period. One of the most common rates to use as the basis for applying interest rates is the London Inter-bank Offered Rate, or LIBOR

a. Disposal tax effect
b. Money market
c. Moneylender
d. Floating interest rate

44. The United States federal _____ is a refundable tax credit. For tax year 2008, a claimant with one qualifying child can receive a maximum credit of $2,917. For two or more qualifying children, the maximum credit is $4,824.
   a. AD-IA Model
   b. Earned Income Tax Credit
   c. ACCRA Cost of Living Index
   d. ACEA agreement

45. The term _____ describes two different concepts:

   - The first is a recognition of partial payment already made towards taxes due.
   - The second is a state benefit paid to workers through the tax system, which has the effect of increasing (rather than reducing) net income.

Within the Australian, Canadian, United Kingdom, and United States tax systems, a _____ is a recognition of partial payment already made towards taxes due. A similar concept exists (fr:Avoir fiscal) in the French tax system. This situation arises, for example, when standard rate tax has been deducted at source , but the tax-payer is subject to further taxation at a higher rate. It also applies in dividend imputation systems.

   a. Tax Credit
   b. 1921 recession
   c. 100-year flood
   d. 130-30 fund

Chapter 16. Public Finance: The Economics of Taxation

1. _____s is the social science that studies the production, distribution, and consumption of goods and services. The term _____s comes from the Ancient Greek οἰκονομία from οἶκος (oikos, 'house') + νόμος (nomos, 'custom' or 'law'), hence 'rules of the house(hold)'. Current _____ models developed out of the broader field of political economy in the late 19th century, owing to a desire to use an empirical approach more akin to the physical sciences.

 a. Economic   b. Inflation
 c. Energy economics   d. Opportunity cost

2. _____ is a branch of economics that deals with the performance, structure, and behavior of a national or regional economy as a whole. Along with microeconomics, _____ is one of the two most general fields in economics. It is the study of the behavior and decision-making of entire economies.

 a. Nominal value   b. New Trade Theory
 c. Macroeconomics   d. Tobit model

3. _____ is a branch of economics that studies how individuals, households and firms and some states make decisions to allocate limited resources, typically in markets where goods or services are being bought and sold. _____ examines how these decisions and behaviours affect the supply and demand for goods and services, which determines prices; and how prices, in turn, determine the supply and demand of goods and services.

Whereas macroeconomics involves the 'sum total of economic activity, dealing with the issues of growth, inflation and unemployment, and with national economic policies relating to these issues' and the effects of government actions on them.

 a. Countercyclical   b. Recession
 c. New Keynesian economics   d. Microeconomics

4. _____ is the study of economic issues concerning the public sector (including government) and its interface with the private sector (including households, businesses, and markets) in a mixed economy. While much of economics is based on how markets work, _____ considers the functioning of government and its role and scope in promoting economic well-being.

Broad methods and topics include:

- analysis and design of public policy
- public-finance theory and its application
- distributional effects of taxation and government expenditures
- analysis of market failure and government failure.

Emphasis is on analytical and scientific methods and normative-ethical analysis, as distinguished from ideology. Examples of topics covered are tax incidence, optimal taxation, the theory of public goods.

 a. Financial economics   b. Macroeconomics
 c. Nominal value   d. Public economics

5. _____ is a field of economics concerned with paying for collective or governmental activities, and with the administration and design of those activities. The field is often divided into questions of what the government or collective organizations should do or are doing, and questions of how to pay for those activities. The broader term (public economics) and the narrower term (government finance) are also often used.

Chapter 16. Public Finance: The Economics of Taxation

a. Value capture
b. Minimum Municipal Obligation
c. Tax increment financing
d. Public finance

6. To _____ is to impose a financial charge or other levy upon a taxpayer by a state or the functional equivalent of a state.

_____es are also imposed by many subnational entities. _____es consist of direct _____ or indirect _____, and may be paid in money or as its labour equivalent (often but not always unpaid.)

a. 1921 recession
b. 130-30 fund
c. 100-year flood
d. Tax

7. To tax is to impose a financial charge or other levy upon a taxpayer by a state or the functional equivalent of a state.

_____ are also imposed by many subnational entities. _____ consist of direct tax or indirect tax, and may be paid in money or as its labour equivalent (often but not always unpaid.)

a. 1921 recession
b. 100-year flood
c. 130-30 fund
d. Taxes

8. A _____ is a tax by which the tax rate increases as the taxable amount increases. 'Progressive' describes a distribution effect on income or expenditure, referring to the way the rate progresses from low to high, where the average tax rate is less than the marginal tax rate. It can be applied to individual taxes or to a tax system as a whole; a year, multi-year, or lifetime.
a. Progressive tax
b. 100-year flood
c. 130-30 fund
d. Proportional tax

9. A _____ is a tax imposed so that the tax rate is fixed as the amount subject to taxation increases. In simple terms, it imposes an equal burden (relative to resources) on the rich and poor. 'Proportional' describes a distribution effect on income or expenditure, referring to the way the rate remains consistent (does not progress from 'low to high' or 'high to low' as income or consumption changes), where the marginal tax rate is equal to the average tax rate.
a. Proportional tax
b. 130-30 fund
c. Regressive tax
d. 100-year flood

10. _____ is the portion of income that is the subject of taxation according to the laws that determine what is income and the taxation rate for that income. Generally, _____ refers to an individual's (or corporation's) gross income, adjusted for various deductions allowable by statute. The main questions put by most individuals in any jurisdiction are 'what makes up my _____' and what tax rates should be applied such that I can work out my tax liability to the state.
a. Taxable income
b. 1921 recession
c. 100-year flood
d. 130-30 fund

11. A _____ is a tax imposed in such a manner that the tax rate decreases as the amount subject to taxation increases. In simple terms, a _____ imposes a greater burden (relative to resources) on the poor than on the rich -- there is an inverse relationship between the tax rate and the taxpayer's ability to pay as measured by assets, consumption, or income. 'Regressive' describes a distribution effect on income or expenditure, referring to the way the rate progresses from high to low, where the average tax rate exceeds the marginal tax rate.

a. 130-30 fund
b. 100-year flood
c. Proportional tax
d. Regressive tax

12. A _____ is a consumption tax charged at the point of purchase for certain goods and services. The tax is usually set as a percentage by the government charging the tax. There is usually a list of exemptions.
   a. 130-30 fund
   b. 1921 recession
   c. 100-year flood
   d. Sales tax

13. _____ was a survey conducted by the U.S. Department of Justice to gauge the prevalence of alcohol and illegal drug use among prior arrestees. It was a reformulation of the prior Drug Use Forecasting (DUF) program, focused on five drugs in particular: cocaine, marijuana, methamphetamine, opiates, and PCP.

Participants were randomly selected from arrest records in major metropolitan areas; because no personally identifying information is taken from each record chosen, the resulting data can be correlated to arrest rates, but not to the total population of persons charged.

   a. Arrestee Drug Abuse Monitoring
   b. AD-IA Model
   c. ACEA agreement
   d. ACCRA Cost of Living Index

14. _____ was a Scottish moral philosopher and a pioneer of political economy. One of the key figures of the Scottish Enlightenment, Smith is the author of The Theory of Moral Sentiments and An Inquiry into the Nature and Causes of the Wealth of Nations. The latter, usually abbreviated as The Wealth of Nations, is considered his magnum opus and the first modern work of economics.
   a. Adolph Fischer
   b. Adolf Hitler
   c. Alan Greenspan
   d. Adam Smith

15. _____ is the concept or idea of fairness in economics, particularly as to taxation or welfare economics.

In welfare economics, _____ may be distinguished from economic efficiency in overall evaluation of social welfare. Although '_____' has broader uses, it may be posed as a counterpart to economic inequality in yielding a 'good' distribution of welfare.

   a. Equity
   b. AD-IA Model
   c. ACCRA Cost of Living Index
   d. ACEA agreement

16. _____ is a common concept in economics, and gives rise to derived concepts such as consumer debt. Generally _____ is defined by opposition to production. But the precise definition can vary because different schools of economists define production quite differently.
   a. Federal Reserve Bank Notes
   b. Cash or share options
   c. Foreclosure data providers
   d. Consumption

17. In business, _____ is the total liabilitiess minus total outside assets of an individual or a company. For a company, this is called shareholders' prefernce and may be referred to as book value. _____ is stated as at a particular year in time.

Chapter 16. Public Finance: The Economics of Taxation

a. Post earnings announcement drift
b. Bond credit rating
c. Net worth
d. Sinking fund

18. Inheritance tax, _____ and death duty are the names given to various taxes which arise on the death of an individual. It is a tax on the estate, or total value of the money and property, of a person who has died. In international tax law, there is a distinction between an _____ and an inheritance tax: the former taxes the personal representatives of the deceased, while the latter taxes the beneficiaries of the estate.
   a. ACCRA Cost of Living Index
   b. Estate tax
   c. AD-IA Model
   d. ACEA agreement

19. In economics, a _____ is the tax on money or property that one living person gives to another. See Gift (law) #Taxation or _____ in the United States.
   a. Taxation as slavery
   b. Gift tax
   c. Fiscal drag
   d. Succession duty

20. In economics, _____ is the analysis of the effect of a particular tax on the distribution of economic welfare. _____ is said to 'fall' upon the group that, at the end of the day, bears the burden of the tax. The key concept is that the _____ or tax burden does not depend on where the revenue is collected, but on the price elasticity of demand and price elasticity of supply.
   a. 130-30 fund
   b. 100-year flood
   c. 1921 recession
   d. Tax incidence

21. The supply of labor is the number of total hours that workers wish to work at a given real wage rate.

    _____ curves are derived from the 'labor-leisure' trade-off. More hours worked earn higher incomes but necessitate a cut in the amount of leisure that workers enjoy.

   a. Labor supply
   b. Creative capitalism
   c. Human trafficking
   d. Late capitalism

22. In a company, _____ is the sum of all financial records of salaries, wages, bonuses and deductions.

A paycheck, is traditionally a paper document issued by an employer to pay an employee for services rendered. While most commonly used in the United States, recently the physical paycheck has been increasingly replaced by electronic direct deposit to bank accounts.

   a. Tax expense
   b. 100-year flood
   c. Total Expense Ratio
   d. Payroll

23. In neoclassical economics and microeconomics, _____ describes the perfect being a market in which there are many small firms, all producing homogeneous goods. In the short term, such markets are productively inefficient as output will not occur where mc is equal to ac, but allocatively efficient, as output under _____ will always occur where mc is equal to mr, and therefore where mc equals ar. However, in the long term, such markets are both allocatively and productively efficient.

Chapter 16. Public Finance: The Economics of Taxation

a. Co-operative economics
c. General equilibrium
b. Perfect competition
d. Law of supply

24. Economics:

- _____, the desire to own something and the ability to pay for it
- _____ curve, a graphic representation of a _____ schedule
- _____ deposit, the money in checking accounts
- _____ pull theory, the theory that inflation occurs when _____ for goods and services exceeds existing supplies
- _____ schedule, a table that lists the quantity of a good a person will buy it each different price
- _____ side economics, the school of economics at believes government spending and tax cuts open economy by raising _____

a. Production
c. McKesson ' Robbins scandal
b. Demand
d. Variability

25. In economics, the _____ can be defined as the graph depicting the relationship between the price of a certain commodity, and the amount of it that consumers are willing and able to purchase at that given price. It is a graphic representation of a demand schedule. The _____ for all consumers together follows from the _____ of every individual consumer: the individual demands at each price are added together.
   a. Demand curve
   c. Wage curve
   b. Cost curve
   d. Kuznets curve

26. In economics, _____ is the ratio of the percent change in one variable to the percent change in another variable. It is a tool for measuring the responsiveness of a function to changes in parameters in a relative way. Commonly analyzed are _____ of substitution, price and wealth.
   a. ACCRA Cost of Living Index
   c. Elasticity
   b. ACEA agreement
   d. Elasticity of demand

27. In economics, a _____ exists when a specific individual or enterprise has sufficient control over a particular product or service to determine significantly the terms on which other individuals shall have access to it. Monopolies are thus characterized by a lack of economic competition for the good or service that they provide and a lack of viable substitute goods. The verb 'monopolize' refers to the process by which a firm gains persistently greater market share than what is expected under perfect competition.
   a. 100-year flood
   c. 1921 recession
   b. 130-30 fund
   d. Monopoly

28. The _____ consists of a number of economic theories which describe the nature of the firm, company including its existence, its behaviour, and its relationship with the market.

Chapter 16. Public Finance: The Economics of Taxation

In simplified terms, the _____ aims to answer these questions:

1. Existence - why do firms emerge, why are not all transactions in the economy mediated over the market?
2. Boundaries - why the boundary between firms and the market is located exactly there? Which transactions are performed internally and which are negotiated on the market?
3. Organization - why are firms structured in such specific way? What is the interplay of formal and informal relationships?

Despite looking simple, these questions are not answered by the established economic theory, which usually views firms as given, and treats them as black boxes without any internal structure.

The First World War period saw a change of emphasis in economic theory away from industry-level analysis which mainly included analysing markets to analysis at the level of the firm, as it became increasingly clear that perfect competition was no longer an adequate model of how firms behaved. Economic theory till then had focussed on trying to understand markets alone and there had been little study on understanding why firms or organisations exist.

a. Policy Ineffectiveness Proposition
b. Theory of the firm
c. Technology gap
d. Khazzoom-Brookes postulate

29. A _____ is a type of business entity in which partners (owners) share with each other the profits or losses of the business _____s are often favored over corporations for taxation purposes, as the _____ structure does not generally incur a tax on profits before it is distributed to the partners (i.e. there is no dividend tax levied.) However, depending on the _____ structure and the jurisdiction in which it operates, owners of a _____ may be exposed to greater personal liability than they would as shareholders of a corporation.

For a country-by-country listing of types of _____s, companies, etc., see Types of business entity.

a. Due diligence
b. Partnership
c. Feoffee
d. Minimum wage law

30. A _____, or simply proprietorship is a type of business entity which legally has no separate existence from its owner. Hence, the limitations of liability enjoyed by a corporation and limited liability partnerships do not apply to sole proprietors. All debts of the business are debts of the owner.

a. Golden hello
b. Corporate tax
c. Golden parachute
d. Sole proprietorship

31. CÄ"terÄ«s paribus is a Latin phrase, literally translated as 'with other things the same.' It is commonly rendered in English as 'all other things being equal.' A prediction, or a statement about causal or logical connections between two states of affairs, is qualified by _____ in order to acknowledge, and to rule out, the possibility of other factors which could override the relationship between the antecedent and the consequent.

A _____ assumption is often fundamental to the predictive purpose of scientific inquiry. In order to formulate scientific laws, it is usually necessary to rule out factors which interfere with examining a specific causal relationship.

a. Friedman-Savage utility function
b. Dematerialization
c. Capital outflow
d. Ceteris paribus

32. _____ is the study of how best to design a tax to avoid distortion and inefficiency. Other things being equal, if a tax-payer must choose between two mutually exclusive economic projects (say investments) that face the same pre-tax risk and returns, the one with the lower tax or with a tax break would be chosen by the rational actor. With that insight, economists argue that generally taxes distort behavior.

a. Indirect tax
b. Olivera-Tanzi effect
c. Optimal tax
d. Optimal tax theory

33. _____ theory is the study of how best to design a tax to avoid distortion and inefficiency. Other things being equal, if a tax-payer must choose between two mutually exclusive economic projects (say investments) that face the same pre-tax risk and returns, the one with the lower tax or with a tax break would be chosen by the rational actor. With that insight, economists argue that generally taxes distort behavior.

a. Olivera-Tanzi effect
b. Optimal tax theory
c. Optimal Tax
d. User charge

34. The _____ of 2003 ('JGTRRA', Pub.L. 108-27, 117 Stat. 752), was passed by the United States Congress on May 23, 2003 and signed by President Bush on May 28, 2003.

Among other provisions, the act accelerated certain tax changes passed in the Economic Growth and Tax Relief Reconciliation Act of 2001, increased the exemption amount for the individual Alternative Minimum Tax, and lowered taxes of income from dividends and capital gains.

a. 1921 recession
b. 130-30 fund
c. 100-year flood
d. Jobs and Growth Tax Relief Reconciliation Act

Chapter 17. International Trade, Comparative Advantage, and Protectionism

1. In economics, an _____ is any good or commodity, transported from one country to another country in a legitimate fashion, typically for use in trade. _____ goods or services are provided to foreign consumers by domestic producers. _____ is an important part of international trade.
   - a. ACEA agreement
   - b. AD-IA Model
   - c. Export
   - d. ACCRA Cost of Living Index

2. In economics, an _____ is any good (e.g. a commodity) or service brought into one country from another country in a legitimate fashion, typically for use in trade. It is a good that is brought in from another country for sale. _____ goods or services are provided to domestic consumers by foreign producers. An _____ in the receiving country is an export to the sending country.
   - a. Import
   - b. Import quota
   - c. Incoterms
   - d. Economic integration

3. In economics, _____ refers to the ability of a party to produce a good or service using fewer real resources than another entity producing the same good or service..A party has an _____ when using the same input as another party, it can produce a greater output. Since _____ is determined by a simple comparison of labor productivities, it is possible for a a party to have no _____ in anything. It can be contrasted with the concept of comparative advantage which refers to the ability to produce a particular good at a lower opportunity cost.
   - a. International economics
   - b. ACCRA Cost of Living Index
   - c. Index number
   - d. Absolute advantage

4. In economics, _____ refers to the ability of a person or a country to produce a particular good at a lower marginal cost and opportunity cost than another person or country. It is the ability to produce a product most efficiently given all the other products that could be produced. It can be contrasted with absolute advantage which refers to the ability of a person or a country to produce a particular good at a lower absolute cost than another.
   - a. Comparative advantage
   - b. Triffin dilemma
   - c. Hot money
   - d. Gravity model of trade

5. _____ in its literal sense is the process of transformation of local or regional phenomena into global ones. It can be described as a process by which the people of the world are unified into a single society and function together.

   This process is a combination of economic, technological, sociocultural and political forces.
   - a. Globally Integrated Enterprise
   - b. Global Cosmopolitanism
   - c. Helsinki Process on Globalisation and Democracy
   - d. Globalization

6. The _____ were import tariffs designed to support domestic British corn prices against competition from less expensive foreign imports between 1815 and 1846. The tariffs were introduced by the Importation Act 1815 (55 Geo. 3 c. 26) and repealed by the Importation Act 1846 (9 ' 10 Vict. c. 22). These laws are often viewed as examples of British mercantilism, and their abolition marked a significant step towards free trade.
   - a. Federal Reserve Police
   - b. Holder in due course
   - c. Nexus of contracts
   - d. Corn Laws

7. _____s is the social science that studies the production, distribution, and consumption of goods and services. The term _____s comes from the Ancient Greek oá¼°κονομῖα from oá¼¶κος (oikos, 'house') + νÏŒμος (nomos, 'custom' or 'law'), hence 'rules of the house(hold)'. Current _____ models developed out of the broader field of political economy in the late 19th century, owing to a desire to use an empirical approach more akin to the physical sciences.

a. Economic
b. Opportunity cost
c. Energy economics
d. Inflation

8. The _____ was a period in the late 18th and early 19th centuries when major changes in agriculture, manufacturing, mining, and transportation had a profound effect on the socioeconomic and cultural conditions in Britain. The changes subsequently spread throughout Europe, North America, and eventually the world. The onset of the _____ marked a major turning point in human society; almost every aspect of daily life was eventually influenced in some way.
   a. Industrial Revolution
   b. Adolf Hitler
   c. Adam Smith
   d. Adolph Fischer

9. _____ originally was the term for studying production, buying and selling, and their relations with law, custom, and government. _____ originated in moral philosophy. It developed in the 18th century as the study of the economies of states -- polities, hence _____.
   a. Geoeconomics
   b. Productive and unproductive labour
   c. Dirigisme
   d. Political Economy

10. _____ by John Stuart Mill was the most important economics or political economy textbook of the mid nineteenth century. It was revised until its seventh edition in 1871, shortly before Mill's death in 1873, and republished in numerous other editions.

Mill's Principles were written in a style of prose far flung from the introductory texts of today.

   a. The Rise and Fall of the Great Powers
   b. Limits to Growth
   c. Principles of Political Economy and Taxation
   d. Principles of Political Economy

11. On the _____ is a book by David Ricardo on economics. The book concludes that land rent grows as population increases. It also clearly lays out the theory of comparative advantage, which shows that all nations can benefit from free trade, even if a nation lacks an absolute advantage in all sectors of its economy.
   a. Principles of Political Economy and Taxation
   b. The Wealth of Nations
   c. Butterfly Economics
   d. Theory of Moral Sentiments

12. _____ is exchange of capital, goods, and services across international borders or territories. In most countries, it represents a significant share of gross domestic product (GDP.) While _____ has been present throughout much of history, its economic, social, and political importance has been on the rise in recent centuries.
   a. Incoterms
   b. Intra-industry trade
   c. Import license
   d. International trade

13. In microeconomics, _____ is quite simply the conversion of inputs into outputs. It is an economic process that uses resources to create a good or service that is suitable for exchange. This can include manufacturing, storing, shipping, and packaging.
   a. MET
   b. Red Guards
   c. Solved
   d. Production

14. In finance, the _____s between two currencies specifies how much one currency is worth in terms of the other. It is the value of a foreign natione;s currency in terms of the home natione;s currency. For example an _____ of 102 Japanese yen to the United States dollar means that JPY 102 is worth the same as USD 1.

a. ACCRA Cost of Living Index
b. ACEA agreement
c. Interbank market
d. Exchange rate

15. In international economics and international trade, _____ or _____ is the relative prices of a country's export to import. '_____' are sometimes used as a proxy for the relative social welfare of a country, but this heuristic is technically questionable and should be used with extreme caution. An improvement in a nation's _____ is good for that country in the sense that it has to pay less for the products it import.
   a. Terms of trade
   b. Common market
   c. Commercial invoice
   d. Kennedy Round

16. In economics a country's _____ is commonly understood as the amount of land, labor, capital, and entrepreneurship that a country possesses and can exploit for manufacturing. Countries with a large endowment of resources tend to be more prosperous than those with a small endowment, all other things being equal. The development of sound institutions to access and equitably distribute these resources, however, is necessary in order for a country to obtain the greatest benefit from its _____.
   a. Factor endowment
   b. Price scissors
   c. Dutch disease
   d. Foreign Affiliate Trade Statistics

17. The _____ is one of the four critical theorems of the Heckscher-Ohlin model. It states: 'A capital-abundant country will export the capital-intensive good, while the labor-abundant country will export the labor-intensive good.'

The critical assumption of the Heckscher-Ohlin model is that the two countries are identical, except for the difference in resource endowments. This also implies that the aggregate preferences are the same.

   a. No-trade theorem
   b. Stolper-Samuelson theorem
   c. Heckscher-Ohlin theorem
   d. 100-year flood

18. _____ was a Swedish economist and politician. He was a professor of economics at the Stockholm School of Economics from 1929 to 1965. He was also leader of the People's Party, a social-liberal party which at the time was the largest party in opposition to the governing Social Democratic Party, from 1944 to 1967.
   a. Bertil Gotthard Ohlin
   b. Maximilian Carl Emil Weber
   c. Martin Luther
   d. Nicholas II

19. An _____ is a governmental subsidy paid to farmers and agribusinesses to supplement their income, manage the supply of agricultural commodities, and influence the cost and supply of such commodities. Examples of such commodities include wheat, feed grains (grain used as fodder, such as maize, sorghum, barley, and oats), cotton, milk, rice, peanuts, sugar, tobacco, and oilseeds such as soybeans.

The European Union use agricultural subsidies to encourage self-sufficiency

Agricultural subsidies to European farmers and fisheries make up more than 40 percent of the EU budget.

   a. ACCRA Cost of Living Index
   b. Agricultural subsidy
   c. AD-IA Model
   d. ACEA agreement

Chapter 17. International Trade, Comparative Advantage, and Protectionism

20. A _____ is a duty imposed on goods when they are moved across a political boundary. They are usually associated with protectionism, the economic policy of restraining trade between nations. For political reasons, _____s are usually imposed on imported goods, although they may also be imposed on exported goods.
    a. 130-30 fund
    b. 1921 recession
    c. 100-year flood
    d. Tariff

21. Competition law, known in the United States as _____ law, has three main elements:

    - prohibiting agreements or practices that restrict free trading and competition between business entities. This includes in particular the repression of cartels.
    - banning abusive behaviour by a firm dominating a market, or anti-competitive practices that tend to lead to such a dominant position. Practices controlled in this way may include predatory pricing, tying, price gouging, refusal to deal, and many others.
    - supervising the mergers and acquisitions of large corporations, including some joint ventures. Transactions that are considered to threaten the competitive process can be prohibited altogether, or approved subject to 'remedies' such as an obligation to divest part of the merged business or to offer licences or access to facilities to enable other businesses to continue competing.

    The substance and practice of competition law varies from jurisdiction to jurisdiction. Protecting the interests of consumers (consumer welfare) and ensuring that entrepreneurs have an opportunity to compete in the market economy are often treated as important objectives. Competition law is closely connected with law on deregulation of access to markets, state aids and subsidies, the privatisation of state owned assets and the establishment of independent sector regulators. In recent decades, competition law has been viewed as a way to provide better public services.

    a. Anti-Inflation Act
    b. United Kingdom competition law
    c. Intellectual property law
    d. Antitrust

22. _____ is the concept of adding accumulated interest back to the principal, so that interest is earned on interest from that moment on. The act of declaring interest to be principal is called compounding (i.e., interest is compounded.) A loan, for example, may have its interest compounded every month: in this case, a loan with $100 principal and 1% interest per month would have a balance of $101 at the end of the first month.
    a. Fama-French three factor model
    b. Compound interest
    c. General purpose technologies
    d. Foreclosure data providers

23. _____ is a term used to describe how different aspects between economies are integrated. The basics of this theory were written by the Hungarian Economist Béla Balassa in the 1960s. As _____ increases, the barriers of trade between markets diminishes.
    a. Economic integration
    b. Import license
    c. Inward investment
    d. Import

24. The _____ was the outcome of the failure of negotiating governments to create the International Trade Organization (ITO.) GATT was formed in 1947 and lasted until 1994, when it was replaced by the World Trade Organization. The Bretton Woods Conference had introduced the idea for an organization to regulate trade as part of a larger plan for economic recovery after World War II.

a. General Agreement on Trade in Services
b. Dutch-Scandinavian Economic Pact
c. General Agreement on Tariffs and Trade
d. GATT

25. _____ is the practice of selling a product or service at a very low price, intending to drive competitors out of the market, or create barriers to entry for potential new competitors. If competitors or potential competitors cannot sustain equal or lower prices without losing money, they go out of business or choose not to enter the business. The predatory merchant then has fewer competitors or is even a de facto monopoly, and can then raise prices above what the market would otherwise bear.
    a. Group boycott
    b. Predatory pricing
    c. Third line forcing
    d. Restraint of trade

26. _____ is one of the four Ps of the marketing mix. The other three aspects are product, promotion, and place. It is also a key variable in microeconomic price allocation theory.
    a. Pricing
    b. Premium pricing
    c. Guaranteed Maximum Price
    d. Point of total assumption

27. The _____ provided for the negotiation of tariff agreements between the United States and separate nations, particularly Latin American countries. It resulted in a reduction of duties.

President Franklin D. Roosevelt was authorized by the Act for a fixed period of time to negotiate on bilateral basis with other countries and then implement reductions in tariffs in exchange for compensating tariff reductions by the partner trading country. Roosevelt was also instructed to maximize market access abroad without jeopardizing domestic industry, and reduce tariffs only as necessary to promote exports in accord with the 'needs of various branches of American production.' A most favored nation clause was also included.

    a. Patent Law Treaty
    b. Reciprocal Trade Agreements Act
    c. Long service leave
    d. Kaldor-Hicks efficiency

28.

The _____ was the first United States Federal statute to limit cartels and monopolies. It falls under antitrust law.

The Act provides: 'Every contract, combination in the form of trust or otherwise, or conspiracy, in restraint of trade or commerce among the several States, or with foreign nations, is declared to be illegal'. The Act also provides: 'Every person who shall monopolize, or attempt to monopolize, or combine or conspire with any other person or persons, to monopolize any part of the trade or commerce among the several States, or with foreign nations, shall be deemed guilty of a felony [. . .]' The Act put responsibility upon government attorneys and district courts to pursue and investigate trusts, companies and organizations suspected of violating the Act. The Clayton Act extended the right to sue under the antitrust laws to 'any person who shall be injured in his business or property by reason of anything forbidden in the antitrust laws.' Under the Clayton Act, private parties may sue in U.S. district court and should they prevail, they may be awarded treble damages and the cost of suit, including reasonable attorney's fees.

Chapter 17. International Trade, Comparative Advantage, and Protectionism

a. 130-30 fund
c. 100-year flood
b. 1921 recession
d. Sherman Antitrust Act

29. The _____ was an act signed into law on June 17, 1930, that raised U.S. tariffs on over 20,000 imported goods to record levels. In the United States 1,028 economists signed a petition against this legislation, and after it was passed, many countries retaliated with their own increased tariffs on U.S. goods, and American exports and imports were reduced by more than half.

Although rated capacity had increased tremendously, actual output, income, and expenditure had not.

a. Judgment summons
c. Smoot-Hawley Tariff Act
b. Patent Law Treaty
d. Loss of use

30. The _____ of 1974 (actually enacted January 3, 1975 as Pub.L. 93-618, 88 Stat. 1978, 19 U.S.C. ch.12) was passed to help industry in the United States become more competitive or phase workers into other industries or occupations. It created fast track authority for the President to negotiate trade agreements that Congress can approve or disapprove but cannot amend or filibuster. The fast track authority created under the Act extended to 1994 and was restored in 2002 by the _____ of 2002.

a. 100-year flood
c. 130-30 fund
b. 1921 recession
d. Trade Act

31. The _____ commenced in September 1986 and continued until April 1994. The round, based on the General Agreement on Tariffs and Trade (GATT) ministerial meeting in Geneva (1982), was launched in Punta del Este in Uruguay (hence the name), followed by negotiations in Montreal, Geneva, Brussels, Washington, D.C., and Tokyo, with the 20 agreements finally being signed in Marrakech - the Marrakesh Agreement. The Round transformed the GATT into the World Trade Organization.

a. ACEA agreement
c. AD-IA Model
b. ACCRA Cost of Living Index
d. Uruguay Round

32. _____ is a fee paid on borrowed assets. It is the price paid for the use of borrowed money, or, money earned by deposited funds. Assets that are sometimes lent with _____ include money, shares, consumer goods through hire purchase, major assets such as aircraft, and even entire factories in finance lease arrangements.

a. Internal debt
c. Asset protection
b. Insolvency
d. Interest

33. The _____ is an economic and political union of 27 member states, located primarily in Europe. It was established by the Treaty of Maastricht on 1 November 1993, upon the foundations of the pre-existing European Economic Community. With a population of almost 500 million, the _____ generates an estimated 30% share (US$18.4 trillion in 2008) of the nominal gross world product.

a. European Court of Justice
c. ACCRA Cost of Living Index
b. ACEA agreement
d. European Union

34. _____ is a type of trade policy that allows traders to act and transact without interference from government. Thus, the policy permits trading partners mutual gains from trade, with goods and services produced according to the theory of comparative advantage.

Under a _____ policy, prices are a reflection of true supply and demand, and are the sole determinant of resource allocation.

- a. 100-year flood
- b. Free Trade
- c. 130-30 fund
- d. 1921 recession

35. The _____ is a trilateral trade bloc in North America created by the governments of the United States, Canada, and Mexico. The agreement creating the trade bloc came into force on January 1, 1994. It superseded the Canada-United States Free Trade Agreement between the U.S. and Canada.
- a. Case-Shiller Home Price Indices
- b. Federal Reserve Bank Notes
- c. Demand-side technologies
- d. North American Free Trade Agreement

36. In economics, a _____ exists when a specific individual or enterprise has sufficient control over a particular product or service to determine significantly the terms on which other individuals shall have access to it. Monopolies are thus characterized by a lack of economic competition for the good or service that they provide and a lack of viable substitute goods. The verb 'monopolize' refers to the process by which a firm gains persistently greater market share than what is expected under perfect competition.
- a. 100-year flood
- b. 1921 recession
- c. 130-30 fund
- d. Monopoly

Chapter 18. Globalization

1. In economics, the term _____ of income or _____ refers to a simple economic model which describes the reciprocal circulation of income between producers and consumers. In the _____ model, the inter-dependent entities of producer and consumer are referred to as 'firms' and 'households' respectively and provide each other with factors in order to facilitate the flow of income. Firms provide consumers with goods and services in exchange for consumer expenditure and 'factors of production' from households.
   a. 130-30 fund
   b. 100-year flood
   c. 1921 recession
   d. Circular flow

2. _____ in its literal sense is the process of transformation of local or regional phenomena into global ones. It can be described as a process by which the people of the world are unified into a single society and function together.

   This process is a combination of economic, technological, sociocultural and political forces.

   a. Helsinki Process on Globalisation and Democracy
   b. Globally Integrated Enterprise
   c. Global Cosmopolitanism
   d. Globalization

3. _____s is the social science that studies the production, distribution, and consumption of goods and services. The term _____s comes from the Ancient Greek oá¼°κονομῐα from oá¼¶κος (oikos, 'house') + vΐŒμος (nomos, 'custom' or 'law'), hence 'rules of the house(hold)'. Current _____ models developed out of the broader field of political economy in the late 19th century, owing to a desire to use an empirical approach more akin to the physical sciences.
   a. Inflation
   b. Opportunity cost
   c. Energy economics
   d. Economic

4. _____ can be defined as the process of increasing economic integration between two countries, leading to the emergence of a global marketplace or a single world market. Depending on the paradigm, globalization can be viewed as both a positive and a negative phenomenon.

   Whilst _____ has been occurring for the last several thousand years (since the emergence of trans-national trade), it has begun to occur at an increased rate over the last 20-30 years.

   a. Economic secession
   b. Anarcho-capitalism
   c. Autarchism
   d. Economic Globalization

5. The _____ of monetary management established the rules for commercial and financial relations among the world's major industrial states in the mid 20th Century. The _____ was the first example of a fully negotiated monetary order intended to govern monetary relations among independent nation-states.

   Preparing to rebuild the international economic system as World War II was still raging, 730 delegates from all 44 Allied nations gathered at the Mount Washington Hotel in Bretton Woods, New Hampshire, United States, for the United Nations Monetary and Financial Conference.

   a. 130-30 fund
   b. 1921 recession
   c. 100-year flood
   d. Bretton Woods system

Chapter 18. Globalization

6. _____, 1st Baron Keynes was a renowned economist from Britain whose many ideas on economic and political theories as well as on many governments' monetary policies influenced America. He advocated a government that played an active role in the lives of people regarding business, economy, etc. In this role, the government would use fiscal measures to reduce the consequences of recessions, economic depressions and booms.
   a. Adolf Hitler
   b. Adam Smith
   c. John Maynard Keynes
   d. Adolph Fischer

7. In economics, _____ refers to the ability of a person or a country to produce a particular good at a lower marginal cost and opportunity cost than another person or country. It is the ability to produce a product most efficiently given all the other products that could be produced. It can be contrasted with absolute advantage which refers to the ability of a person or a country to produce a particular good at a lower absolute cost than another.
   a. Comparative advantage
   b. Triffin dilemma
   c. Gravity model of trade
   d. Hot money

8. _____ is a type of trade policy that allows traders to act and transact without interference from government. Thus, the policy permits trading partners mutual gains from trade, with goods and services produced according to the theory of comparative advantage.

   Under a _____ policy, prices are a reflection of true supply and demand, and are the sole determinant of resource allocation.

   a. 100-year flood
   b. 130-30 fund
   c. 1921 recession
   d. Free Trade

9. The _____ was the outcome of the failure of negotiating governments to create the International Trade Organization (ITO.) GATT was formed in 1947 and lasted until 1994, when it was replaced by the World Trade Organization. The Bretton Woods Conference had introduced the idea for an organization to regulate trade as part of a larger plan for economic recovery after World War II.
   a. Dutch-Scandinavian Economic Pact
   b. General Agreement on Tariffs and Trade
   c. General Agreement on Trade in Services
   d. GATT

10. The _____ is a trilateral trade bloc in North America created by the governments of the United States, Canada, and Mexico. The agreement creating the trade bloc came into force on January 1, 1994. It superseded the Canada-United States Free Trade Agreement between the U.S. and Canada.
    a. North American Free Trade Agreement
    b. Demand-side technologies
    c. Case-Shiller Home Price Indices
    d. Federal Reserve Bank Notes

11. A _____ is a duty imposed on goods when they are moved across a political boundary. They are usually associated with protectionism, the economic policy of restraining trade between nations. For political reasons, _____s are usually imposed on imported goods, although they may also be imposed on exported goods.
    a. 100-year flood
    b. 1921 recession
    c. 130-30 fund
    d. Tariff

Chapter 18. Globalization

12. In economics, _____ refers to the ability of a party to produce a good or service using fewer real resources than another entity producing the same good or service..A party has an _____ when using the same input as another party, it can produce a greater output. Since _____ is determined by a simple comparison of labor productivities, it is possible for a a party to have no _____ in anything. It can be contrasted with the concept of comparative advantage which refers to the ability to produce a particular good at a lower opportunity cost.

   a. ACCRA Cost of Living Index
   b. International economics
   c. Index number
   d. Absolute advantage

13. An _____ is a governmental subsidy paid to farmers and agribusinesses to supplement their income, manage the supply of agricultural commodities, and influence the cost and supply of such commodities. Examples of such commodities include wheat, feed grains (grain used as fodder, such as maize, sorghum, barley, and oats), cotton, milk, rice, peanuts, sugar, tobacco, and oilseeds such as soybeans.

   The European Union use agricultural subsidies to encourage self-sufficiency

   Agricultural subsidies to European farmers and fisheries make up more than 40 percent of the EU budget.

   a. AD-IA Model
   b. Agricultural subsidy
   c. ACCRA Cost of Living Index
   d. ACEA agreement

14. The _____ is an important selective, mainly private, international organization designed by its founders to supervise and liberalize international trade. The organization officially commenced on 1 January 1995, under the Marrakesh Agreement, succeeding the 1947 General Agreement on Tariffs and Trade (GATT.)

   The _____ deals with regulation of trade between participating countries; it provides a framework for negotiating and formalising trade agreements, and a dispute resolution process aimed at enforcing participants' adherence to _____ agreements which are signed by representatives of member governments and ratified by their parliaments.

   a. Bio-energy village
   b. 2009 G-20 London summit protests
   c. Backus-Kehoe-Kydland consumption correlation puzzle
   d. World Trade Organization

15. _____ is an organized social movement and market-based approach that aims to help producers in developing countries and promote sustainability. The movement advocates the payment of a 'fair price' as well as social and environmental standards in areas related to the production of a wide variety of goods. It focuses in particular on exports from developing countries to developed countries, most notably handicrafts, coffee, cocoa, sugar, tea, bananas, honey, cotton, wine, fresh fruit, chocolate and flowers.

   a. Fair trade
   b. 100-year flood
   c. 130-30 fund
   d. 1921 recession

16. _____ to the arrival of new individuals into a habitat or population. It is a biological concept and is important in population ecology, differentiated from emigration and migration.

   _____ is a modern phenomenon.

a. AD-IA Model
b. ACCRA Cost of Living Index
c. Immigration
d. ACEA agreement

17. The _____ is a US private, nonprofit research organization dedicated to studying the science and empirics of economics, especially the American economy. It is 'committed to undertaking and disseminating unbiased economic research among public policymakers, business professionals, and the academic community.' It publishes NBER Working Papers and books. The NBER is located in Cambridge, Massachusetts with branch offices in Palo Alto, California, and New York City.
   a. National Bureau of Economic Research
   b. Deutsche Bank
   c. CEFTA
   d. Non-governmental organization

18. The _____ is an international financial institution that provides financial and technical assistance to developing countries for development programs (e.g. bridges, roads, schools, etc.) with the stated goal of reducing poverty.

The _____ differs from the _____ Group, in that the _____ comprises only two institutions:

- International Bank for Reconstruction and Development (IBRD)
- International Development Association (IDA)

Whereas the latter incorporates these two in addition to three more:

- International Finance Corporation (IFC)
- Multilateral Investment Guarantee Agency (MIGA)
- International Centre for Settlement of Investment Disputes (ICSID)

John Maynard Keynes (right) represented the UK at the conference, and Harry Dexter White represented the US.

The _____ is one of two major financial institutions created as a result of the Bretton Woods Conference in 1944. The International Monetary Fund, a related but separate institution, is the second.

   a. Flow to Equity-Approach
   b. World Bank
   c. Bank-State-Branch
   d. Financial costs of the 2003 Iraq War

19. The _____, also Simpson-Mazzoli Act (Pub.L. 99-603, 100 Stat. 3359, signed by President Ronald Reagan on November 6, 1986) is an Act of Congress which reformed United States immigration law. The Act made it illegal to knowingly hire or recruit illegal immigrants (immigrants who do not possess lawful work authorization), required employers to attest to their employees' immigration status, and granted amnesty to certain illegal immigrants who entered the United States before January 1, 1982 and had resided there continuously.
   a. Immigration Reform and Control Act
   b. Intellectual property
   c. Unreported employment
   d. Insurance law

20. In general _____ refers to any non-human asset made by humans and then used in production. Often, it refers to economic capital in some ambiguous combination of infrastructural capital and natural capital. As these are combined in process-specific and firm-specific ways that neoclassical macroeconomics does not differentiate at its level of analysis, it is common to refer only to physical vs. human capital and seek so-called 'balanced growth' that develops both in tandem

Such analyses, however, fails to make distinctions considered critical by many modern economists.

    a. Linkage principle
    b. Factor cost
    c. Net domestic product
    d. Physical capital

21. _____ refers to a business or organization attempting to acquire goods or services to accomplish the goals of the enterprise. Though there are several organizations that attempt to set standards in the _____ process, processes can vary greatly between organizations. Typically the word '_____' is not used interchangeably with the word 'procurement', since procurement typically includes Expediting, Supplier Quality, and Traffic and Logistics (T'L) in addition to _____.

    a. 100-year flood
    b. 130-30 fund
    c. Purchasing
    d. Free port

22. The _____ is an international organization that oversees the global financial system by following the macroeconomic policies of its member countries, in particular those with an impact on exchange rates and the balance of payments. It is an organization formed to stabilize international exchange rates and facilitate development. It also offers financial and technical assistance to its members, making it an international lender of last resort.

    a. ACCRA Cost of Living Index
    b. ACEA agreement
    c. Office of Thrift Supervision
    d. International Monetary Fund

23. _____ is a term that has become widely accepted for referring to a legally constituted, people from _____ created by natural or legal persons with no participation or representation of any government. In the cases in which NGOs are funded totally or partially by governments, the NGO maintains its non-governmental status therefore it excludes government representatives from membership in the organization. Unlike the term intergovernmental organization, '_____' is a term in generalized use but not a legal definition, in many jurisdictions these type of organizations are defined as 'civil society organizations' or alternative terms.

    a. Citizens for an Alternative Tax System
    b. Non-governmental organization
    c. Bankruptcy of Lehman Brothers
    d. Great Leap Forward

24. In economics, a _____ is a good that is non-rivaled and non-excludable. This means, respectively, that consumption of the good by one individual does not reduce availability of the good for consumption by others; and that no one can be effectively excluded from using the good. In the real world, there may be no such thing as an absolutely non-rivaled and non-excludable good; but economists think that some goods approximate the concept closely enough for the analysis to be economically useful.

    a. Neoclassical synthesis
    b. Happiness economics
    c. Demand-pull theory
    d. Public good

25. _____ can be generally defined as the course of action or inaction taken by governmental entities with regard to a particular issue or set of issues. Other scholars define it as a system of 'courses of action, regulatory measures, laws, and funding priorities concerning a given topic promulgated by a governmental entity or its representatives.' _____ is commonly embodied 'in constitutions, legislative acts, and judicial decisions.'

In the United States, this concept refers not only to the end result of policies, but more broadly to the decision-making and analysis of governmental decisions. _____ is also considered an academic discipline, as it is studied by professors and students at _____ schools of major universities throughout the country.

Chapter 18. Globalization

a. Public policy
c. 100-year flood
b. 130-30 fund
d. 1921 recession

26. _____ are defined as public goods that could be delivered as private goods, but are usually delivered by the government for various reasons, including social policy, and finances from public funds like taxes.

Common examples of public goods include: defense and law enforcement (including the system of property rights), public fireworks, lighthouses, clean air and other environmental goods, and information goods, such as software development, authorship, and invention.

a. Common property
c. Government monopoly
b. Collective goods
d. Privatizing profits and socializing losses

27. A _____ is an object whose consumption increases the utility of the consumer, for which the quantity demanded exceeds the quantity supplied at zero price. _____s are usually modeled as having diminishing marginal utility. The first individual purchase has high utility; the second has less.
a. Composite good
c. Merit good
b. Good
d. Pie method

28. _____ is a branch of economics that deals with the performance, structure, and behavior of a national or regional economy as a whole. Along with microeconomics, _____ is one of the two most general fields in economics. It is the study of the behavior and decision-making of entire economies.
a. Tobit model
c. Nominal value
b. New Trade Theory
d. Macroeconomics

29. _____ is a branch of economics that studies how individuals, households and firms and some states make decisions to allocate limited resources, typically in markets where goods or services are being bought and sold. _____ examines how these decisions and behaviours affect the supply and demand for goods and services, which determines prices; and how prices, in turn , determine the supply and demand of goods and services.

Whereas macroeconomics involves the 'sum total of economic activity, dealing with the issues of growth, inflation and unemployment, and with national economic policies relating to these issues' and the effects of government actions on them.

a. New Keynesian economics
c. Recession
b. Microeconomics
d. Countercyclical

30. The term _____ was initially coined in 1989 by John Williamson to describe a set of ten specific economic policy prescriptions that he considered should constitute the 'standard' reform package promoted for crisis-wracked developing countries by Washington, DC-based institutions such as the International Monetary Fund (IMF), World Bank and the US Treasury Department.

Subsequently, as Williamson himself has pointed out, the term has come to be used in a different and broader sense, as a synonym for market fundamentalism; in this broader sense, Williamson states, it has been criticized by people such as George Soros and Nobel Laureate Joseph E. Stiglitz. The _____ is also criticized by others such as some Latin American politicians and heterodox economists.

a. Secular basis
b. Minimum wage
c. Washington Consensus
d. Permanent income hypothesis

31. _____ is a branch of economics with three main subdisciplines international trade, monetary economics and international finance.

- International trade studies goods-and-services flows across international boundaries from supply-and-demand factors, economic integration, and policy variables such as tariff rates and trade quotas.
- International finance studies the flow of capital across international financial markets, and the effects of these movements on exchange rates.
- International monetary economics and macroeconomics studies money and macro flows across countries.

- Stanley W. Black (2008.) 'international monetary institutions,' The New Palgrave Dictionary of Economics. 2nd Edition.

a. International Economics
b. Economic depreciation
c. Index number
d. ACCRA Cost of Living Index

32. _____ is an economic system in which wealth, and the means of producing wealth, are privately owned. Through _____, the land, labor, and capital are owned, operated, and traded for the purpose of generating profits, without force or fraud, by private individuals either singly or jointly, and investments, distribution, income, production, pricing and supply of goods, commodities and services are determined by voluntary private decision in a market economy. A distinguishing feature of _____ is that each person owns his or her own labor and therefore is allowed to sell the use of it to employers.
a. Late capitalism
b. Capitalism
c. Socialism for the rich and capitalism for the poor
d. Creative capitalism

33. An _____ or Å"conomic system is a system that involves the production, distribution and consumption of goods and services between the entities in a particular society. It is the method used by society to produce and distribute goods and services. The _____ is composed of people and institutions, including their relationships to productive resources, such as through the convention of property.
a. Information economy
b. Economic system
c. Intention economy
d. Indicative planning

34. _____ is a term used to describe a policy of allowing events to take their own course. The term is a French phrase literally meaning 'let do'. It is a doctrine that states that government generally should not intervene in the marketplace.
a. Communization
b. Laissez-faire
c. Heroic capitalism
d. Theory of Productive Forces

35. _____ in political thought refers to economic theories of social organization advocating collective ownership and administration of the means of production and distribution of goods, and a society characterized by equality for all individuals, with an egalitarian method of compensation. Modern _____ originated in the late 19th-century intellectual and working class political movement that criticized the effects of industrialization and private ownership on society. Karl Marx posited that _____ would be achieved via class struggle and a proletarian revolution after a transitional stage from capitalism called the dictatorship of the proletariat.
a. Adolf Hitler
b. Adam Smith
c. Adolph Fischer
d. Socialism

Chapter 19. Economic Growth in Developing and Transitional Economies

1. _____s is the social science that studies the production, distribution, and consumption of goods and services. The term _____s comes from the Ancient Greek οἰκονομῑα from οἶκος (oikos, 'house') + νόμος (nomos, 'custom' or 'law'), hence 'rules of the house(hold)'. Current _____ models developed out of the broader field of political economy in the late 19th century, owing to a desire to use an empirical approach more akin to the physical sciences.
   a. Energy economics
   b. Opportunity cost
   c. Inflation
   d. Economic

2. The _____ is the central banking system of the United States. Created in 1913 by the enactment of the Federal Reserve Act (signed by Woodrow Wilson), it is a quasi-public and quasi-private (government entity with private components) banking system that comprises (1) the presidentially appointed Board of Governors of the _____ in Washington, D.C.; (2) the Federal Open Market Committee; (3) twelve regional Federal Reserve Banks located in major cities throughout the nation acting as fiscal agents for the U.S. Treasury, each with its own nine-member board of directors; (4) numerous other private U.S. member banks, which subscribe to required amounts of non-transferable stock in their regional Federal Reserve Banks; and (5) various advisory councils. Since February 2006, Ben Bernanke has served as the Chairman of the Board of Governors of the _____.
   a. Monetary Policy Report to the Congress
   b. Federal Reserve System
   c. Term auction facility
   d. Federal Reserve System Open Market Account

3. _____ is the development of economic wealth of countries or regions for the well-being of their inhabitants. It is the process by which a nation improves the economic, political, and social well being of its people. From a policy perspective, _____ can be defined as efforts that seek to improve the economic well-being and quality of life for a community by creating and/or retaining jobs and supporting or growing incomes and the tax base.
   a. Economic methodology
   b. Economic development
   c. Inflation
   d. Experimental economics

4. _____ is a term used in economic research and policy debates. As with freedom generally, there are various definitions, but no universally accepted concept of _____. One major approach to _____ comes from the libertarian tradition emphasizing free markets and private property, while another extends the welfare economics study of individual choice, with greater _____ coming from a 'larger' (in some technical sense) set of possible choices.
   a. Economic liberalization
   b. Investment policy
   c. International sanctions
   d. Economic freedom

5. The _____ or gross domestic income (GDI), a basic measure of an economy's economic performance, is the market value of all final goods and services produced within the borders of a nation in a year. _____ can be defined in three ways, all of which are conceptually identical. First, it is equal to the total expenditures for all final goods and services produced within the country in a stipulated period of time (usually a 365-day year.)
   a. Monopolistic competition
   b. Gross domestic product
   c. Market structure
   d. Countercyclical

6. _____ comprises the total value produced within a country (i.e. its gross domestic product), together with its income received from other countries (notably interest and dividends), less similar payments made to other countries.

The _____ consists of: the personal consumption expenditures, the gross private investment, the government consumption expenditures, the net income from assets abroad (net income receipts), and the gross exports of goods and services, after deducting two components: the gross imports of goods and services, and the indirect business taxes. The _____ is similar to the gross national product (GNP), except that in measuring the GNP one does not deduct the indirect business taxes.

a. Base period
b. Central limit order book
c. Gross national income
d. Market-based instruments

7. _____ is the shortage of common things such as food, clothing, shelter and safe drinking water, all of which determine the quality of life. It may also include the lack of access to opportunities such as education and employment which aid the escape from _____ and/or allow one to enjoy the respect of fellow citizens. According to Mollie Orshansky who developed the _____ measurements used by the U.S. government, 'to be poor is to be deprived of those goods and services and pleasures which others around us take for granted.' Ongoing debates over causes, effects and best ways to measure _____, directly influence the design and implementation of _____-reduction programs and are therefore relevant to the fields of public administration and international development.

a. Growth Elasticity of Poverty
b. Liberal welfare reforms
c. Poverty map
d. Poverty

8. _____ is a categorical label used to describe states that are considered to be underdeveloped in terms of their economy or level of industrialization, globalization, standard of living, health, education or other criteria for 'advancements'.

_____ was a reference to the 'the Third Estate, the commoners of France before and during the French Revolution, opposed to the priests and nobles who composed the First Estate and the Second Estate.

a. 2008 budget crisis
b. Bulgarian-American trade
c. Third World
d. Developed markets

9. _____ has several particular meanings:

- in mathematics
  - _____ function
  - Euler _____
  - _____
  - _____ subgroup
  - method of _____ s (partial differential equations)
- in physics and engineering
  - any _____ curve that shows the relationship between certain input- and output parameters, e.g.
  - an I-V or current-voltage _____ is the current in a circuit as a function of the applied voltage
  - Receiver-Operator _____
- in fiction
  - in Dungeons ' Dragons, _____ is another name for ability score

a. Russian financial crisis
b. Characteristic
c. Demand
d. Technocracy

10. A variety of measures of _____ and output are used in economics to estimate total economic activity in a country or region, including gross domestic product (GDP), gross national product (GNP), and net _____

Chapter 19. Economic Growth in Developing and Transitional Economies 139

There are three main ways of calculating these numbers; the output approach, the income approach and the expenditure approach. In theory, the three must yield the same, because total expenditures on goods and services must equal the total income paid to the producers (Gnational income), and that must also equal the total value of the output of goods and services (GNP.)

a. National income
b. Gross world product
c. Volume index
d. GNI per capita

11. _____ is a misspelled phrase from Latin 'pro capite' phrase meaning per head with pro meaning 'per' or 'for each' and capite meaning 'head.' Both words together equate to the phrase 'for each head.'

It is usually used in the field of statistics to indicate the average per person for any given concern, such as income, crime rate, etc.

It is also used in wills to indicate that each of the named beneficiaries should receive, by devise or bequest, equal shares of the estate. This is in contrast to a per stirpes division, in which each branch of the inheriting family inherits an equal share of the estate.

a. Sargan test
b. Population statistics
c. False positive rate
d. Per capita

12. _____, in economics, occurs when assets and/or money rapidly flow out of a country, due to an economic event that disturbs investors and causes them to lower their valuation of the assets in that country, or otherwise to lose confidence in its economic strength. This leads to a disappearance of wealth and is usually accompanied by a sharp drop in the exchange rate of the affected country (depreciation in a variable exchange rate regime, or a forced devaluation in a fixed exchange rate regime.)

This fall is particularly damaging when the capital belongs to the people of the affected country, because not only are the citizens now burdened by the loss of faith in the economy and devaluation of their currency, but probably also their assets have lost much of their nominal value.

a. Liquid capital
b. Capital formation
c. Firm-specific infrastructure
d. Capital flight

13. _____ is a term used in national accounts statistics and macroeconomics. It basically refers to the net additions to the (physical) capital stock in an accounting period, or, to the value of the increase of the capital stock; though it may occasionally also refer to the (growth of the) total stock of capital formed.

Thus, in UNSNA, _____ equals fixed capital investment, the increase in the value of inventories held, plus (net) lending to foreign countries, during an accounting period.

a. Consumption of fixed capital
b. Capital intensity
c. Capital formation
d. Capital flight

Chapter 19. Economic Growth in Developing and Transitional Economies

14. _____ or human capital flight is a large emigration of individuals with technical skills or knowledge, normally due to conflict, lack of opportunity, political instability, or health risks. _____ is usually regarded as an economic cost, since emigrants usually take with them the fraction of value of their training sponsored by the government. It is a parallel of capital flight which refers to the same movement of financial capital.
   a. 100-year flood
   b. 130-30 fund
   c. 1921 recession
   d. Brain drain

15. An _____ is a person who has possession of an enterprise and assumes significant accountability for the inherent risks and the outcome. It is an ambitious leader who combines land, labor, and capital to create and market new goods or services. The term is a loanword from French and was first defined by the Irish economist Richard Cantillon.
   a. ACCRA Cost of Living Index
   b. Entrepreneur
   c. ACEA agreement
   d. Expansionary policies

16. In business, _____, Overhead cost or _____ expense refers to an ongoing expense of operating a business. The term _____ is usually used to group expenses that are necessary to the continued functioning of the business, but do not directly generate profits.

    _____ expenses are all costs on the income statement except for direct labor and direct materials.

   a. ACEA agreement
   b. ACCRA Cost of Living Index
   c. AD-IA Model
   d. Overhead

17. In economics, an _____ is any good or commodity, transported from one country to another country in a legitimate fashion, typically for use in trade. _____ goods or services are provided to foreign consumers by domestic producers. _____ is an important part of international trade.
   a. ACCRA Cost of Living Index
   b. ACEA agreement
   c. AD-IA Model
   d. Export

18. In economics, an _____ is any good (e.g. a commodity) or service brought into one country from another country in a legitimate fashion, typically for use in trade.It is a good that is brought in from another country for sale. _____ goods or services are provided to domestic consumers by foreign producers. An _____ in the receiving country is an export to the sending country.
   a. Incoterms
   b. Economic integration
   c. Import quota
   d. Import

19. _____ industrialization is a trade and economic policy based on the premise that a country should attempt to reduce its foreign dependency through the local production of industrialized products. Adopted in many Latin American countries from the 1930s until the late 1980s, and in some Asian and African countries from the 1950s on, Import substitutionl was theoretically organized in the works of Raúl Prebisch, Hans Singer, Celso Furtado and other structural economic thinkers, and gained prominence with the creation of the United Nations Economic Commission for Latin America and the Caribbean . Insofar as its suggestion of state-induced industrialization through governmental spending, it is largely influenced by Keynesian thinking, as well as the infant industry arguments adopted by some highly industrialized countries, such as the United States, until the 1940s.
   a. ACCRA Cost of Living Index
   b. ACEA agreement
   c. AD-IA Model
   d. Import substitution

Chapter 19. Economic Growth in Developing and Transitional Economies

20. An _____ is a governmental subsidy paid to farmers and agribusinesses to supplement their income, manage the supply of agricultural commodities, and influence the cost and supply of such commodities. Examples of such commodities include wheat, feed grains (grain used as fodder, such as maize, sorghum, barley, and oats), cotton, milk, rice, peanuts, sugar, tobacco, and oilseeds such as soybeans.

The European Union use agricultural subsidies to encourage self-sufficiency

Agricultural subsidies to European farmers and fisheries make up more than 40 percent of the EU budget.

   a. AD-IA Model
   b. Agricultural subsidy
   c. ACCRA Cost of Living Index
   d. ACEA agreement

21. _____ can be defined as the process of increasing economic integration between two countries, leading to the emergence of a global marketplace or a single world market. Depending on the paradigm, globalization can be viewed as both a positive and a negative phenomenon.

Whilst _____ has been occurring for the last several thousand years (since the emergence of trans-national trade), it has begun to occur at an increased rate over the last 20-30 years.

   a. Economic secession
   b. Anarcho-capitalism
   c. Autarchism
   d. Economic globalization

22. The _____ is an international organization that oversees the global financial system by following the macroeconomic policies of its member countries, in particular those with an impact on exchange rates and the balance of payments. It is an organization formed to stabilize international exchange rates and facilitate development. It also offers financial and technical assistance to its members, making it an international lender of last resort.

   a. Office of Thrift Supervision
   b. International Monetary Fund
   c. ACEA agreement
   d. ACCRA Cost of Living Index

23. _____ is a term used to describe the policy changes implemented by the International Monetary Fund (IMF) and the World Bank (the Bretton Woods Institutions) in developing countries. These policy changes are conditions (Conditionalities) for getting new loans from the IMF or World Bank, or for obtaining lower interest rates on existing loans. Conditionalities are implemented to ensure that the money lent will be spent in accordance with the overall goals of the loan.

   a. 130-30 fund
   b. 100-year flood
   c. Regional development
   d. Structural adjustment

24. The _____ is an international financial institution that provides financial and technical assistance to developing countries for development programs (e.g. bridges, roads, schools, etc.) with the stated goal of reducing poverty.

The _____ differs from the _____ Group, in that the _____ comprises only two institutions:

- International Bank for Reconstruction and Development (IBRD)
- International Development Association (IDA)

Chapter 19. Economic Growth in Developing and Transitional Economies

Whereas the latter incorporates these two in addition to three more:

- International Finance Corporation (IFC)
- Multilateral Investment Guarantee Agency (MIGA)
- International Centre for Settlement of Investment Disputes (ICSID)

John Maynard Keynes (right) represented the UK at the conference, and Harry Dexter White represented the US.

The _____ is one of two major financial institutions created as a result of the Bretton Woods Conference in 1944. The International Monetary Fund, a related but separate institution, is the second.

a. World Bank
b. Bank-State-Branch
c. Flow to Equity-Approach
d. Financial costs of the 2003 Iraq War

25. _____ is the increase in the amount of the goods and services produced by an economy over time. It is conventionally measured as the percent rate of increase in real gross domestic product, or real GDP. Growth is usually calculated in real terms, i.e. inflation-adjusted terms, in order to net out the effect of inflation on the price of the goods and services produced.

a. ACEA agreement
b. ACCRA Cost of Living Index
c. AD-IA Model
d. Economic growth

26. _____ in its literal sense is the process of transformation of local or regional phenomena into global ones. It can be described as a process by which the people of the world are unified into a single society and function together.

This process is a combination of economic, technological, sociocultural and political forces.

a. Global Cosmopolitanism
b. Globally Integrated Enterprise
c. Helsinki Process on Globalisation and Democracy
d. Globalization

27. _____ is the change in population over time, and can be quantified as the change in the number of individuals in a population using 'per unit time' for measurement. The term _____ can technically refer to any species, but almost always refers to humans, and it is often used informally for the more specific demographic term _____ rate, and is often used to refer specifically to the growth of the population of the world.

Simple models of _____ include the Malthusian Growth Model and the logistic model.

a. Population dynamics
b. 100-year flood
c. 130-30 fund
d. Population growth

28. _____, or a _____ is the concept of a resulting effect (cf. cause and effect, arising from another action. In general terms, it is used to indicate that all human actions, particularly crime and sin, have profound effects.

a. Solved
b. Consequence
c. Variability
d. Rule

29. In statistics, the _____ problem occurs when one considers a set of statistical inferences simultaneously. Errors in inference, including confidence intervals that fail to include their corresponding population parameters are more likely to occur when one considers the family as a whole. Several statistical techniques have been developed to prevent this from happening, allowing significance levels for single and _____ to be directly compared.
   a. Multiple comparisons
   b. Hypotheses suggested by the data
   c. Familywise error rate
   d. False discovery rate

30. _____ is the planning of when to have children, and the use of birth control and other techniques to implement such plans. Other techniques commonly used include sexuality education, prevention and management of sexually transmitted infections, pre-conception counseling and management, and infertility management.

    _____ is sometimes used as a synonym for the use of birth control, though it often includes more.

   a. Helix of sustainability
   b. Sustainable advertising
   c. Family planning
   d. Reconciliation ecology

31. _____ is a measure of the number of deaths (in general scaled to the size of that population, per unit time. _____ is typically expressed in units of deaths per 1000 individuals per year; thus, a _____ of 9.5 in a population of 100,000 would mean 950 deaths per year in that entire population. It is distinct from morbidity rate, which refers to the number of individuals in poor health during a given time period (the prevalence rate) or the number who currently have that disease (the incidence rate), scaled to the size of the population.
   a. 130-30 fund
   b. Mortality rate
   c. 1921 recession
   d. 100-year flood

32. Necessary _____s:

If x is a necessary _____ of y, then the presence of y necessarily implies the presence of x. The presence of x, however, does not imply that y will occur.

Sufficient _____s:

If x is a sufficient _____ of y, then the presence of x necessarily implies the presence of y.

   a. Philosophy of economics
   b. Political philosophy
   c. Materialism
   d. Cause

33. _____ is that which is owed; usually referencing assets owed, but the term can also cover moral obligations and other interactions not requiring money. In the case of assets, _____ is a means of using future purchasing power in the present before a summation has been earned. Some companies and corporations use _____ as a part of their overall corporate finance strategy.
   a. Hard money loan
   b. Debt
   c. Collateral Management
   d. Debenture

Chapter 19. Economic Growth in Developing and Transitional Economies

34. _____ is the lengthening the time of debt repayment and forgiving part of the loan for a date. .
a. Demand deposit
b. Debt rescheduling
c. Clawbacks in economic development
d. Tangible Common Equity

35. The _____ is a regional organization whose participating countries are former Soviet Republics.

The CIS is comparable to a confederation similar to the original European Community. Although the CIS has few supranational powers, it is more than a purely symbolic organization, possessing coordinating powers in the realm of trade, finance, lawmaking, and security.

a. 130-30 fund
b. 100-year flood
c. Commonwealth of Independent States
d. 1921 recession

36. _____ to the arrival of new individuals into a habitat or population. It is a biological concept and is important in population ecology, differentiated from emigration and migration.

_____ is a modern phenomenon.

a. ACEA agreement
b. ACCRA Cost of Living Index
c. AD-IA Model
d. Immigration

37. _____ is an economic system in which wealth, and the means of producing wealth, are privately owned. Through _____, the land, labor, and capital are owned, operated, and traded for the purpose of generating profits, without force or fraud, by private individuals either singly or jointly, and investments, distribution, income, production, pricing and supply of goods, commodities and services are determined by voluntary private decision in a market economy. A distinguishing feature of _____ is that each person owns his or her own labor and therefore is allowed to sell the use of it to employers.
a. Socialism for the rich and capitalism for the poor
b. Late capitalism
c. Capitalism
d. Creative capitalism

38. _____ is a socioeconomic structure and political ideology that promotes the establishment of an egalitarian, classless, stateless society based on common ownership and control of the means of production and property in general. In political science, the term '_____' is sometimes used to refer to communist states, a form of government in which the state operates under a one-party system and declares allegiance to Marxism-Leninism or a derivative thereof, even if the party does not actually claim that it has already reached _____.

Forerunners of communist ideas existed in antiquity and particularly in the 18th and early 19th century France, with thinkers such as Jean-Jacques Rousseau and the more radical Gracchus Babeuf.

a. New Communist Movement
b. Democratic centralism
c. Communism
d. Social fascism

39. A _____ is a system of politics and government. It is usually compared to the law system, economic system, cultural system, and other social systems. It is different from them, and can be generally defined on a spectrum from left, e.g. communism, to the right, e.g. fascism.

a. 100-year flood
c. 130-30 fund
b. 1921 recession
d. Political system

40. In economics, a _____ is a good that is non-rivaled and non-excludable. This means, respectively, that consumption of the good by one individual does not reduce availability of the good for consumption by others; and that no one can be effectively excluded from using the good. In the real world, there may be no such thing as an absolutely non-rivaled and non-excludable good; but economists think that some goods approximate the concept closely enough for the analysis to be economically useful.
   a. Neoclassical synthesis
   c. Happiness economics
   b. Public good
   d. Demand-pull theory

41. _____ in political thought refers to economic theories of social organization advocating collective ownership and administration of the means of production and distribution of goods, and a society characterized by equality for all individuals, with an egalitarian method of compensation. Modern _____ originated in the late 19th-century intellectual and working class political movement that criticized the effects of industrialization and private ownership on society. Karl Marx posited that _____ would be achieved via class struggle and a proletarian revolution after a transitional stage from capitalism called the dictatorship of the proletariat.
   a. Adolf Hitler
   c. Adam Smith
   b. Adolph Fischer
   d. Socialism

42. _____s is a broad, and sometimes controversial, term. A normative definition held by many socialists states that all _____ theories and arrangements are united by the desire to produce for use rather than profit, achieve greater equality, give the workers greater control of the means of production and create a more effective mechanism for producing and distributing goods and services within an economy through rational scientific planning, if not directing the economy based on social goals rather than individual profit. Within the limits set by these principles, however, _____s can take many different forms.
   a. Socialist economic
   c. Libertarian perspectives on revolution
   b. Trade Union Unity League
   d. Free-market environmentalism

43. A _____ is an object whose consumption increases the utility of the consumer, for which the quantity demanded exceeds the quantity supplied at zero price. _____s are usually modeled as having diminishing marginal utility. The first individual purchase has high utility; the second has less.
   a. Composite good
   c. Pie method
   b. Merit good
   d. Good

44. _____ or market division schemes are agreements in which competitors divide markets among themselves. In such schemes, competing firms allocate specific customers or types of customers, products, or territories among themselves. For example, one competitor will be allowed to sell to, or bid on contracts let by, certain customers or types of customers.
   a. Discrete choice
   c. History of minimum wage
   b. G-20 Leaders Summit on Financial Markets and the World Economy
   d. Market allocation

45. A _____ is any systematic process enabling many market players to bid and ask: helping bidders and sellers interact and make deals. It is not just the price mechanism but the entire system of regulation, qualification, credentials, reputations and clearing that surrounds that mechanism and makes it operate in a social context.

Because a _____ relies on the assumption that players are constantly involved and unequally enabled, a _____ is distinguished specifically from a voting system where candidates seek the support of voters on a less regular basis.

- a. Price mechanism
- b. Market system
- c. Contestable market
- d. Competitive equilibrium

46. _____ is used to assign the available resources in an economic way. It is part of resource management.

In strategic planning,is a plan for using available resources, for example human resources, especially in the near term, to achieve goals for the future.

- a. 100-year flood
- b. 130-30 fund
- c. 1921 recession
- d. Resource allocation

47. The _____ is the market for securities, where companies and governments can raise longterm funds. It is a market in which money is lent for periods longer than a year. The _____ includes the stock market and the bond market.

- a. Financial instrument
- b. Capital market
- c. Multi-family office
- d. Performance attribution

48.

_____ was the last General Secretary of the Communist Party of the Soviet Union, serving from 1985 until 1991, and also the last head of state of the USSR, serving from 1988 until its collapse in 1991. He was the only Soviet leader to have been born after the October Revolution of 1917.

Gorbachev was born in Stavropol Krai into a peasant family, and operated combine harvesters on collective farms.

- a. Adolf Hitler
- b. Mikhail Sergeyevich Gorbachev
- c. Adolph Fischer
- d. Adam Smith

49. A _____ is an economy based on the division of labor in which the prices of goods and services are determined in a free price system set by supply and demand. This is often contrasted with a planned economy, in which a central government determines the price of goods and services using a fixed price system. Market economies are contrasted with mixed economy where the price system is not entirely free but under some government control that is not extensive enough to constitute a planned economy.

- a. Nutritional Economics
- b. Network Economy
- c. Commons-based peer production
- d. Market economy

50. _____ is a branch of economics that deals with the performance, structure, and behavior of a national or regional economy as a whole. Along with microeconomics, _____ is one of the two most general fields in economics. It is the study of the behavior and decision-making of entire economies.

a. Macroeconomics
b. Nominal value
c. New Trade Theory
d. Tobit model

51. _____ in economics and business is the result of an exchange and from that trade we assign a numerical monetary value to a good, service or asset. If Alice trades Bob 4 apples for an orange, the _____ of an orange is 4 apples. Inversely, the _____ of an apple is 1/4 oranges.
  a. Premium pricing
  b. Price
  c. Price book
  d. Price war

52. _____ is the incidence or process of transferring ownership of a business, enterprise, agency or public service from the public sector (government) to the private sector (business.) In a broader sense, _____ refers to transfer of any government function to the private sector including governmental functions like revenue collection and law enforcement.

The term '_____' also has been used to describe two unrelated transactions.

  a. Ricardian equivalence
  b. Compound empowerment
  c. Performance reports
  d. Privatization

53. In economics, _____ refers to the ability of a party to produce a good or service using fewer real resources than another entity producing the same good or service..A party has an _____ when using the same input as another party, it can produce a greater output. Since _____ is determined by a simple comparison of labor productivities, it is possible for a a party to have no _____ in anything. It can be contrasted with the concept of comparative advantage which refers to the ability to produce a particular good at a lower opportunity cost.
  a. Index number
  b. ACCRA Cost of Living Index
  c. International economics
  d. Absolute advantage

54. In economics, _____ refers to the ability of a person or a country to produce a particular good at a lower marginal cost and opportunity cost than another person or country. It is the ability to produce a product most efficiently given all the other products that could be produced. It can be contrasted with absolute advantage which refers to the ability of a person or a country to produce a particular good at a lower absolute cost than another.
  a. Triffin dilemma
  b. Gravity model of trade
  c. Hot money
  d. Comparative advantage

55. _____ is the removal or simplification of government rules and regulations that constrain the operation of market forces. _____ does not mean elimination of laws against fraud, but eliminating or reducing government control of how business is done, thereby moving toward a more free market.

The stated rationale for '_____' is often that fewer and simpler regulations will lead to a raised level of competitiveness, therefore higher productivity, more efficiency and lower prices overall.

  a. Deregulation
  b. Macroeconomic policy instruments
  c. Fundamental psychological law
  d. Secular basis

Chapter 19. Economic Growth in Developing and Transitional Economies

56. A _____ is a theoretical term that economists use to describe a market which is free from government intervention (i.e. no regulation, no subsidization, no single monetary system and no governmental monopolies.) In a _____, property rights are voluntarily exchanged at a price arranged solely by the mutual consent of sellers and buyers. By definition, buyers and sellers do not coerce each other, in the sense that they obtain each other's property without the use of physical force, threat of physical force, or fraud, nor is the coerced by a third party (such as by government via transfer payments) and they engage in trade simply because they both consent and believe that it is a good enough choice.

   a. Third camp
   b. Delegation
   c. Leninism
   d. Free market

57. _____, in law and economics, is a form of risk management primarily used to hedge against the risk of a contingent loss. _____ is defined as the equitable transfer of the risk of a loss, from one entity to another, in exchange for a premium, and can be thought of as a guaranteed small loss to prevent a large, possibly devastating loss. An insurer is a company selling the _____; an insured or policyholder is the person or entity buying the _____.

   a. ACCRA Cost of Living Index
   b. ACEA agreement
   c. AD-IA Model
   d. Insurance

58. _____ is the belief that changes occur, or ought to occur, slowly in the form of gradual steps

In politics, the concept of _____ is used to describe the belief that change ought to be modified in small, discrete increments rather than abrupt changes such as revolutions or uprisings. _____ is one of the defining features of political conservatism and reformism. According to Machiavellian politics, Congressmen are pushed to agree to _____.

   a. 1921 recession
   b. 100-year flood
   c. 130-30 fund
   d. Gradualism

ANSWER KEY

Chapter 1
1. d   2. d   3. a   4. d   5. b   6. a   7. d   8. b   9. d   10. c
11. d   12. d   13. d   14. b   15. d   16. c   17. c   18. d   19. d   20. d
21. d   22. a   23. d   24. c   25. d   26. a   27. b   28. d   29. a   30. b
31. b   32. d   33. a   34. d   35. d   36. c   37. d   38. b   39. d   40. d
41. d   42. a   43. d   44. a   45. d   46. c   47. d   48. d   49. a   50. a
51. d   52. c   53. d

Chapter 2
1. d   2. b   3. a   4. d   5. a   6. d   7. c   8. a   9. d   10. d
11. d   12. b   13. a   14. d   15. a   16. d   17. d   18. d   19. d   20. a
21. b   22. d   23. d   24. d   25. a   26. d   27. b   28. b   29. c   30. b
31. d   32. a   33. d   34. d   35. b   36. c   37. b   38. d   39. d   40. c

Chapter 3
1. d   2. c   3. d   4. b   5. d   6. c   7. d   8. b   9. d   10. d
11. b   12. d   13. c   14. d   15. d   16. d   17. a   18. d   19. a   20. d
21. c   22. d   23. c   24. d   25. c   26. d   27. d   28. c   29. d   30. d
31. a   32. a   33. a   34. b   35. d   36. d   37. d   38. b   39. c   40. c
41. d

Chapter 4
1. d   2. d   3. c   4. d   5. a   6. b   7. a   8. c   9. d   10. a
11. d   12. c   13. a   14. d   15. d   16. c   17. d   18. d   19. c   20. d
21. d   22. a   23. d   24. c   25. a   26. c   27. c   28. b   29. b   30. c
31. d   32. c   33. d   34. c   35. d   36. c   37. d

Chapter 5
1. a   2. d   3. c   4. d   5. c   6. d   7. c   8. d   9. d   10. c
11. d   12. d   13. b   14. b   15. b   16. c   17. a   18. b   19. d   20. b
21. b   22. a   23. d   24. d   25. d   26. d   27. a   28. b   29. d   30. c
31. d   32. d   33. d   34. b   35. a   36. a

Chapter 6
1. d   2. d   3. c   4. d   5. d   6. a   7. c   8. a   9. a   10. d
11. d   12. d   13. c   14. d   15. d   16. a   17. a   18. d   19. d   20. b
21. d   22. d   23. d   24. b   25. d   26. c   27. a

Chapter 7
1. a   2. d   3. c   4. b   5. d   6. c   7. c   8. c   9. d   10. d
11. d   12. b   13. d   14. a   15. c   16. b   17. d   18. d   19. a   20. d
21. b

Chapter 8
1. c	2. a	3. d	4. b	5. d	6. b	7. b	8. d	9. a	10. a
11. d	12. d	13. b	14. c	15. d	16. a	17. d	18. a	19. d	20. c
21. d	22. d	23. b							

Chapter 9
1. a	2. b	3. d	4. d	5. c	6. d	7. b	8. c	9. d	10. d
11. b	12. b	13. b	14. c	15. b	16. a	17. d	18. d	19. b	20. b
21. d	22. a	23. d	24. d	25. d	26. d	27. d	28. c	29. b	30. d

Chapter 10
1. b	2. d	3. d	4. c	5. a	6. a	7. d	8. d	9. c	10. c
11. d	12. a	13. d	14. a	15. d	16. c	17. d	18. a	19. c	20. d
21. a	22. d	23. c	24. c	25. d	26. d	27. d			

Chapter 11
1. d	2. d	3. c	4. d	5. a	6. c	7. d	8. d	9. c	10. d
11. b	12. c	13. c	14. c	15. d	16. d	17. d	18. d	19. c	20. c
21. c	22. b	23. c	24. c	25. d	26. d	27. a	28. b		

Chapter 12
1. a	2. d	3. b	4. c	5. a	6. d	7. d	8. a	9. b	10. a
11. d	12. b	13. d	14. c	15. c	16. d	17. b	18. a	19. d	20. d
21. d	22. d	23. b	24. d	25. d	26. d	27. d	28. d	29. d	30. d
31. d	32. c	33. d	34. b	35. b	36. d	37. b	38. d	39. b	40. d
41. c	42. c	43. b	44. c	45. d	46. d				

Chapter 13
1. d	2. b	3. d	4. c	5. a	6. d	7. a	8. d	9. d	10. a
11. d	12. d	13. a	14. d	15. c	16. d	17. d	18. b	19. a	20. a
21. b	22. d	23. c	24. c	25. a	26. d	27. b	28. d	29. d	30. d
31. b	32. b	33. a	34. a	35. a	36. d	37. d	38. c	39. b	40. d
41. d	42. b	43. d	44. b						

Chapter 14
1. c	2. a	3. a	4. c	5. a	6. a	7. a	8. d	9. a	10. d
11. d	12. c	13. d	14. d	15. c	16. a	17. a	18. a	19. a	20. a
21. d	22. d	23. a	24. c	25. a	26. b	27. d	28. d	29. d	30. a
31. c	32. b	33. d	34. c	35. d	36. b	37. d	38. d	39. a	40. d
41. b	42. b	43. d	44. c						

ANSWER KEY

Chapter 15
1. c	2. c	3. d	4. d	5. d	6. c	7. a	8. b	9. a	10. d
11. c	12. c	13. d	14. d	15. d	16. d	17. a	18. d	19. d	20. b
21. a	22. a	23. d	24. b	25. a	26. a	27. d	28. d	29. d	30. d
31. d	32. d	33. d	34. c	35. d	36. c	37. a	38. d	39. c	40. d
41. d	42. b	43. d	44. b	45. a					

Chapter 16
1. a	2. c	3. d	4. d	5. d	6. d	7. d	8. a	9. a	10. a
11. d	12. d	13. a	14. d	15. a	16. d	17. c	18. b	19. b	20. d
21. a	22. d	23. b	24. b	25. a	26. c	27. d	28. b	29. b	30. d
31. d	32. d	33. c	34. d						

Chapter 17
1. c	2. a	3. d	4. a	5. d	6. d	7. a	8. a	9. d	10. d
11. a	12. d	13. d	14. d	15. a	16. a	17. c	18. a	19. b	20. d
21. d	22. b	23. a	24. c	25. b	26. a	27. b	28. d	29. c	30. d
31. d	32. d	33. d	34. b	35. d	36. d				

Chapter 18
1. d	2. d	3. d	4. d	5. d	6. c	7. a	8. d	9. b	10. a
11. d	12. d	13. b	14. d	15. a	16. c	17. a	18. b	19. a	20. d
21. c	22. d	23. b	24. d	25. a	26. b	27. b	28. d	29. b	30. c
31. a	32. b	33. b	34. b	35. d					

Chapter 19
1. d	2. b	3. b	4. d	5. b	6. c	7. d	8. c	9. b	10. a
11. d	12. d	13. c	14. d	15. b	16. d	17. d	18. d	19. d	20. b
21. d	22. b	23. d	24. a	25. d	26. d	27. d	28. b	29. a	30. c
31. b	32. d	33. b	34. b	35. c	36. d	37. c	38. c	39. d	40. b
41. d	42. a	43. d	44. d	45. b	46. d	47. b	48. b	49. d	50. a
51. b	52. d	53. d	54. d	55. a	56. d	57. d	58. d		

www.ingramcontent.com/pod-product-compliance
Lightning Source LLC
Chambersburg PA
CBHW082206230426
43672CB00015B/2915